The AMAR CHITRA KATHA FOLKTALES OMNIBUS

HCCB
HARPERCOLLINS CHILDREN'S BOOKS

TIMELESS
Amar Chitra Katha

This collection, first published in 2024 in India by HarperCollins *Children's Books*, includes:
Funny Folktales published in 2021 by HarperCollins *Children's Books*
Amazing Folktales from South Asia published in 2022 by HarperCollins *Children's Books*
Fascinating Stories from India published in 2022 by HarperCollins *Children's Books*
Favourite Indian Folktales published in 2023 by HarperCollins *Children's Books*
An imprint of HarperCollins *Publishers*
Building No 10, Tower A, 4th Floor, DLF Cyber City, Phase II,
Gurugram – 122002

2 4 6 8 10 9 7 5 3 1

P-ISBN: 978-93-6569-601-1
E-ISBN: 978-93-6569-814-5

Cover and inside illustrations: Based on the artwork in the original Amar Chitra Katha comics

Printed and bound at Replika Press Pvt. Ltd.

HarperCollinsIn

MIX
Paper | Supporting responsible forestry
FSC™ C016779

CONTENTS

AMAZING FOLKTALES FROM SOUTH ASIA

WRITTEN BY

CHRISTOPHER BARETTO

CHO-CHO DORJEE

A Story from Bhutan

In a small village of Bhutan, there lived two brothers, Cho-cho and Che-cho Dorjee. Cho-cho was the elder of the two. Both were hardworking and self-sufficient. They only had each other. Everyone in the village talked about their bond.

It was said that one could separate the salt from the ocean but it was not possible to separate the Dorjee brothers.

Cho-cho was lazy, laid-back and a bit slow. He would often take things literally. Che-cho, on the other hand, was extremely clever. He was strong, sharp and quick-witted. Che-cho did try to help his brother become smarter but failed. However, he loved his brother too much to be bothered by it.

Stories about the Dorjee brothers were popular in the entire village.

One day, one of the villagers was walking on a narrow downhill path with his cart. The cart was full of valuable grains to be traded in the nearby village. The villager was whistling and moving along merrily when he suddenly tripped and...

DOOM DHADAK!
AAAAAAAAAAAAAAAAAH!

The cart lost its balance and fell in a ditch! The villager was in shock. He did not know what to do. "Somebody, please help me!"

he tried calling for help. But no one could hear his plea even from a mile away. After trying hard to move the cart for a while, he sat down next to the ditch and began crying helplessly.

Just then, Cho-cho and Che-cho were passing by. Cho-cho asked the crying man, "Is there a problem, Sir?"

The man replied, "I tripped and fell and now my cart is in this ditch."

Cho-cho thought for a while and said, "But, Sir, how did the cart end up in the ditch if you fell?"

The man realised that Cho-cho was not the brightest of the lot and turned to Che-cho. He said, "Young man, you look strong and healthy. Can you please help me pull my cart out of this ditch?"

Che-cho replied, "Sir, don't worry about that."

Che-cho went near the ditch, grabbed the cart

with one hand and said...

HEAVEEEEEEEEEE HO!

And just like that, he pulled the cart out of the ditch. He did not need anybody's help to carry out the task. The villager was impressed and grateful. To return the favour, he gave them a sack of grains and went about his way.

There were many such instances where the wit and strength of one brother and the foolishness of the other was on display.

One day, Che-cho was leaving for the fields as usual. Before leaving home, he said to Cho-cho, "Brother, please prepare a meal for me and deliver it to me sharp at noon. Also, please make sure that the food is clean."

Che-cho was someone who thoroughly washed his vegetables and grains to ensure he ate only the best quality of meals. While Cho-cho knew that, he took his brother's instructions to the next level.

As instructed, Cho-cho began preparing a meal for his brother. He said to himself, "My brother works hard all day at the field, he takes care of me and loves me a lot. I will make him some rice and meat coated generously with chilli. But he will also need something to wash it down. I will carry a cold jug of milk for that." So, he prepared a complete feast made out of love and admiration for his younger brother.

It was almost noon and Cho-cho departed for the fields where his brother worked. He

was happily walking along when suddenly he encountered a pile of cow dung blocking his path. "What is this?" he wondered. Upon further inspection, the not-so-bright Cho-cho decided to get rid of the cow dung that was lying in his way.

He said, "Dear cow dung, I request you to move out of my way." But the cow dung, of course, did not respond. This angered Cho-cho.

He said to the cow dung angrily, "If you will

not move from my path, I will have to move you!" Cho-cho then kept the tray of food aside and picked up a stone. He threw it at the cow dung and

SPLAAAAAAAAAAAAAASH!

The cow dung splashed everywhere and unfortunately, some of it also splattered onto Che-cho's food. That's when Cho-cho

remembered that his brother had asked him to bring him food that was absolutely clean. He began to panic and started thinking of a solution.

After some time, he saw a stream nearby and thought to himself, "Aha! That's it! I'll just wash the food here and take it to Che-cho. The food will be completely clean and my brother will be impressed. However, I must wash each and every grain." And so, Cho-cho did exactly

that. He spent more than two hours at the stream.

Meanwhile, Che-cho's stomach was growling with hunger.

GRRRRRRRRRRRRRRR.

Not being able to deal with his hunger anymore, he decided to look for his brother. Che-cho found him washing his food near the stream. He exclaimed, "Brother! What are you doing?"

The naive Cho-cho innocently replied, "Your lunch was splattered with cow dung. So, I'm just washing it away."

This really angered Che-cho. He thought to himself, "He is truly hopeless. I will have to arrange for my lunch myself."

He then looked at Cho-cho and said to him, "Kind brother, thank you very much for this. But I will take care of my lunch at home. Why don't you do me another favour? Throw this food away and take care of the oxen in the field until I'm back. DO NOT LET THEM MOVE."

Cho-cho smiled and nodded and left for the fields.

The fields were a beautiful sight. For the longest distance, there were only crops. The sky was clear and beautiful. There was a farm nearby, but the animals were allowed to roam freely. They were familiar with the area, and did not need much supervision. One could easily sit back, relax and enjoy the rest of the day basking in the afternoon sun.

In the fields, Cho-cho made sure to keep a keen eye on the oxen. The oxen were mostly motionless except...

SWOOOOOOOOOOOOOOOOSH!

They were swishing their tails to drive away flies. Seeing this, Cho-cho went to the oxen and said to them, "O Mighty Oxen, your master has asked me to make sure that you do not move at all. So, kindly stop swishing your tails!"

The oxen could not understand what Cho-cho was saying and continued to swish their tails, when suddenly...

MOOOOOOOOOOOOOOOO!

The oxen screamed as they felt something grab them by their tails. It was Cho-cho! He was shouting, "STOP! Don't. Move. Your. Tails." The oxen were trying to break free but

Cho-cho was adamant. After all, he was just obeying his brother's command.

To put an end to their swishing, Cho-cho grabbed a rope and tied their tails to their bodies. "This should keep you still," he said. But that only further agitated the oxen. They started prancing around the field. Cho-cho shouted, "Stop it, you mindless animals!" and tried to get a hold of them. But he failed.

He went back to the shed to get some more rope and tied the feet of both the oxen. "There you go," he said proudly. "You thought you were smart, huh?" And to reward himself for a job well done, he proceeded to take a nap in the field.

Che-cho returned a couple of hours later. He was dumbfounded when he saw the helpless oxen. He asked Cho-cho what had happened. Cheerfully, Cho-cho explained the situation to him, "I did exactly what you asked me to do, brother!"

THUMP!

Che-cho slapped his forehead in utter disappointment. He thought to himself, "I cannot take it anymore! I need to run away from Cho-cho. I can no longer live with him."

Later that night, Che-cho started preparing for his escape. He began collecting all the essentials he would need. He got a big trunk and started filling it with clothes, food and money. Cho-cho noticed him packing and thought to himself, "Ah, looks like Che-cho is going somewhere. I want to go with him too!"

And so, after Che-cho went to sleep, Cho-cho took out some of the things from the chest and made space for himself.

The next day, Che-cho was ready to leave. He looked around and could not find Cho-cho anywhere. Seeing that as an opportunity to escape, he picked up the trunk and made a run for it.

He walked across valleys, rivers and mountains. It was a tedious journey. Throughout the journey, he kept thinking about his brother's well-being. He thought to himself, "I need to get to the countryside. Cho-cho will manage to take care of himself. I have left enough resources at his disposal to live a life full of happiness."

As night fell, Che-cho decided to camp on the

hillside. He prepared a fire and began cooking a meal for himself. His thoughts about Cho-cho came back. "I really hope Cho-cho manages to live happily without me. But the real question is, will I be able to live happily without him?"

Soon, he began tearing up. He had spent his entire life taking care of his brother and he was missing him. He began to feel guilty for abandoning his brother. Che-cho got up and walked to the edge of the hill and shouted,

"CHO-CHO! PLEASE FORGIVE ME! I MISS YOU, BROTHER!"

KDAK!

Che-cho's trunk opened and Cho-cho sprang out of it. "I am here, brother," he said cheerfully.

Che-cho was surprised and happy to see him. He hugged him tight and said, "I will never leave you alone again, brother."

They then decided to go home and took care of each other thereafter.

The Helpless Sparrow

A Story from Nepal

There once lived a sparrow in the forests of Nepal. Due to her helpful and nurturing nature, all the other animals called her Mother Sparrow. She lived in a tree that was next to the path that led to the king's palace. Every day she would see several travellers walking towards the palace. She would chirp at them and they would respond in the most delightful manner.

Her eggs had recently hatched, and all the other animals were excited to welcome her baby sparrows. This also meant that she had to hunt for extra food so that her chicks were never hungry.

She would begin her mornings searching for worms and grains. On some days, it was an easy task but on others, she really had to struggle. One day, she searched for hours but could not find a single grain for her young chicks.

Mother Sparrow was in great distress and began to weep. Next to her tree was a colony of ants. One of the ants noticed that she was crying and asked her what had happened. She told him about her situation. The ant immediately ran back to the anthill and returned ten minutes later with some of his friends who were carrying grains on their backs. The ant said to her, "Here, you go. Feed this to your babies."

Mother Sparrow hesitated. The ant urged the sparrow, "Take it. You are a part of this forest.

All of us must help each other." Mother Sparrow accepted the gift. From that day onwards, the sparrow and the ant became best friends.

Often, she would bring some extra food for the ants and help them fend off any threats. The ants would be motivated in the morning with her cheerful chirping and work harder for the colony. There was complete harmony.

One day, Mother Sparrow went out in search of food as usual. On the way, she found a big bean near a pile of mud. She looked at it and said, "Wow! What a big, juicy bean! It is enough to feed all of us." She picked up the bean, washed it in a stream and went back to her nest.

However, all that effort in getting the bean had made the sparrow dirty. She said to herself, "How foolish of me! I cleaned the bean but forgot to clean myself. Better tidy myself up before I call it a day and sit down to eat."

The sparrow went back to the stream to wash herself. After a quick bath, she returned to her nest only to find...

NOOOOOOOOOOOOOOOOOO!

The big juicy bean had disappeared! It was nowhere to be found. After making sure that her chicks were safe, the sparrow decided

to look for the missing bean. She thought to herself, "I can't find it anywhere!

Someone must've stolen it for sure. But who could it be?"

Just then, she saw a carpenter passing by. He was carrying some logs and making his way to the King's palace. "I need to get there in time before the King arrives," he kept mumbling to himself.

The sparrow approached him and asked, "Kind Sir, have you seen my bean?" The man was in his own world. So the sparrow repeated herself. He snapped at her, "Huh? What? What bean? Nobody cares about your stupid bean. Get out of here and leave me alone!"

As the carpenter left, the sparrow thought to herself, "Wow, what a rude and selfish man!"

Not too far away, a soldier was seen approaching from the palace. He carried a sword and had a tense look on his face. The soldier said to himself, "The King's procession must be arriving shortly. I need to be there to ensure maximum security. I could lose my job if I don't make it in time."

The sparrow spotted him. She

went to him and asked about the bean. Upon hearing the bird, the soldier got agitated. He said to her, "You stupid bird! You are bothering me for a bean? I have much bigger things to tend to than search for a tiny bean. Now leave!" The sparrow got startled and left him alone.

Just behind the soldier was a minister. He was known to be a cunning and sly man. He was extremely selfish and abused his power all the time. The self-centred minister never helped anyone. But he was also extremely afraid of the King.

Mother Sparrow went to the minister and said, "O wise Minister, your duty is to look after the people of this kingdom. I am a humble bird, please help me find my bean." The minister looked at the sparrow and laughed.

HAHAHAHAHAHAHAHAHA!

"The only two things in this kingdom that I need to look after are the King and myself," he said in an irritable tone. "Now get out of my sight before I get you arrested for wasting my precious time."

Mother Sparrow flew away and sat on a nearby rock. The sobbing sparrow thought, "No one cares about my bean. Who will help me now?" Sometime later...

TROOM TROOM TROOOOOM!

She heard a loud trumpet sound and looked around to see where it was coming from. She saw the King's procession approach. The King was dressed royally and wore all sorts of jewellery. Riding an elephant, he looked proud and regal. The maidens were showering flowers along the way. The King was followed by musicians and some of his subjects. The soldier and the minister who were leading kept shouting, "MAKE WAY FOR HIS ROYAL HIGHNESS!"

Immediately, there was hope in Mother Sparrow's eyes. She said to herself, "That's it! The King will be able to help me get my

bean back!" She flew to him and said, "Your Majesty, I am a mere sparrow that lives in your kingdom. Please help me out. I have lost my bean and cannot find it. Please help me look for it."

The King heard the sparrow and thought to himself, "What is this bird babbling about? If I just ignore her, maybe she will go away." He continued to ignore the bird.

After several tries, Mother Sparrow gave up. Disheartened, she decided to go back to her nest. On the way, she met her friend, the ant. He was returning back to the anthill with some food. He looked at Mother Sparrow and asked, "Hey, Mother Sparrow! What's bothering you?" The sparrow then shared her woes with him.

The ant smiled and said to her, "Is that all? Don't worry! Let me do something about it."

The ant crawled all the way to the procession, avoiding being stamped on by the crowd. He climbed onto the King's elephant and whispered in his ear, "Listen to me, you big doofus! If you don't want me to crawl all the way inside your ear canal and bite you, tell your King to search

for my friend's bean. Understood?"

The frightened elephant said, "Yikes! Don't do that! I'll do whatever you want."

The elephant stopped and turned towards the King and said, "Hey King! Find the sparrow's bean or else I will throw you off my back. All your subjects will see you on the ground. What would that do to your image? Imagine kings from other kingdoms laughing at you. Your subjects will wonder that if you can't sit on an elephant properly, are you fit to run a kingdom? Would you like your throne to be taken away from you?"

The King was very concerned about his image. He did not want to give his enemies a reason to overthrow his rule and agreed to find Mother Sparrow's bean.

He called the minister and told him, "You! Find that sparrow's bean or I will find someone else to fill your seat from tomorrow onwards. Is that understood?"

The minister, who was very protective of his position, replied, "Your wish is my command, Your Majesty," and got to work.

He got hold of the soldier and told him, "Soldier! We have to make sure that we take care of every single being that lives within this kingdom. Go and help that sparrow find her bean, otherwise I will take that sword of yours and cut off your head with it."

The soldier did not want to get into trouble. He said, "Right away, Sire!" and began

searching for the missing bean. He then found the carpenter who was lurking around to get a glimpse of the King. The soldier caught him and said, "YOU! Leave all your supplies and help this sparrow find her bean." The man obliged.

After searching for a while, the carpenter found the bean near Mother Sparrow's nest. He gave it to her and said, "There you go. This bean must've rolled off the tree." Mother

Sparrow happily took it and went back to her nest.

The ant was waiting for her at the nest. The

sparrow thanked him. The ant said to her, "Have a wonderful meal!"

Mother Sparrow interrupted him and said, "Umm, all this activity has made me dirty again. Do you mind looking after the bean while I quickly tidy myself up?"

The ant replied, "Absolutely! We wouldn't want the whole kingdom searching for it again, would we?"

Kamzang the Clever

A Story from Bhutan

Dorji was a wealthy merchant who lived in the city of Thimphu. Over the years, he had travelled across Bhutan and met different kinds of people. Some were witty, while others were dumb or greedy or those who found happiness in little things. This had made Dorji's understanding of people better. He could merely observe someone for a few minutes and understand their character.

Dorji had a son who was eligible for marriage. His son wanted to take over his business but Dorji believed that he needed someone who could be his constant support and companion. Dorji told him, "Son, I will seek a bride for you. Not only will she be compatible with you, but she will also help you handle the business." Saying this, he set out on his journey.

On the way, Dorji met many people. But knowing his son, he knew that none of the women he came across were the right choice for him. After searching for two months, Dorji finally gave up and decided to return home. But the journey was long and dangerous. On the way, he had to cross mountains, hills, rivers and valleys.

One day, Dorji was crossing a beautiful valley. There was an abundance of flowering trees along the way. It was a mesmerising sight. Dorji noticed a bunch of women plucking flowers from the trees and carefully collecting them in their baskets.

One of the girls amongst the group was extremely attractive. Dorji's attention was immediately drawn to her. She was gentle and elegant. But that was not why Dorji was observing her. She was the only one from the group who was picking up flowers that had fallen from the tree. All the other girls were plucking the flowers straight from the tree. The others seemed not too bothered by her actions as if they were used to them.

Dorji thought to himself, "What a strange girl! Why isn't she picking up fresh flowers straight from the trees like her friends? It doesn't make sense at all." This was the first time someone had left Dorji baffled.

Sometime later, it was nearing sunset. One of the girls went to the young lady and told her, "Kamzang, it's time to go! We need to be home before it gets dark."

Dorji exclaimed, "Aha! So that's her name! Well, I guess I should head home, too." Dorji was

sad that his and Kamzang's paths would not cross again.

Dorji continued his journey and came across a stream on his way. He said to himself, "It's going to get dark soon. I better rest near this freshwater stream." He then set up a camp and prepared a fire and started making a meal for himself and his camel.

As luck would have it, Kamzang and her friends arrived at the same stream. Dorji had managed to get there faster as he was riding a camel. He said to himself, "Oh! That's the same girl. What was her name? That's right! Kamzang!"

The girls had to cross the stream. Before they did that, all the girls removed their shoes and carried them in their hands. All but one. For some odd reason, Kamzang didn't take off her shoes. The girls even tried to convince her but she didn't listen to them. They all then continued to cross the stream.

Dorji thought to himself, "First the odd picking of flowers and now this. What is this young girl up to?" He pondered over her actions all through the night.

The next day, he continued his journey back home. On the way, he came across a small village. He had run out of supplies and needed to restock. One of the villagers told him to go to their town's only shop.

The shop was big and had all sorts of things. There were groceries, travel supplies, decorations, etc. The entire shop was being handled by one man. Dorji went to him and began talking to him. While he bought his supplies, he found out more about the shopkeeper who was also a merchant. The shopkeeper told him, "I have spent my entire life exchanging goods. I am now teaching everything I have learned to my daughter so that she can carry on my legacy."

Dorji was moved by his story. He told the shopkeeper that he was in the same situation. The two of them bonded over their collective experience and knowledge. The shopkeeper said to Dorji, "You must spend the night at my place, friend." At first, Dorji hesitated but then he agreed.

Later that day, at the shopkeeper's house, Dorji got to meet his family and that's when Dorji met his daughter. "Kamzang! "Yo- you! You're Kamzang!" he said to her in a surprised tone.

Everyone in the room was surprised to see that the stranger knew Kamzang.

Dorji explained, "You see, while I was travelling back home, I came across your daughter at the valley where I couldn't help but notice her strange behaviour." He then looked at Kamzang and asked her why she picked flowers off the ground while her friends plucked them from the trees.

"You see, by plucking flowers directly from the trees, we hurt the trees. Moreover, the trees might scratch us with their sharp thorns and bark. Which is why I found it best to pick them up from the ground," she told Dorji.

Dorji was impressed. He thought to himself, "What a considerate girl." He continued, "Then I saw you later that day near the stream. You walked in the water with your shoes whereas your friends took them off. What was the reason for that?"

Kamzang smiled and replied, "Well, that's

simple. While crossing the stream, one doesn't know what lurks in the water. One could get stung by a crab or bitten by a water snake. One could even hurt their foot on a sharp stone. The shoes help prevent that."

Dorji thought, "Wow! She is also extremely intelligent. She is the perfect girl for my son.

They will be able to keep each other happy for the rest of their lives. She will surely bring wealth and prosperity to our family."

The next day, Dorji asked Kamzang's father for her hand in marriage for his son. He agreed as long as his daughter agreed to the match as well. Kamzang wanted to meet Dorji's son. A week later, the two of them met and spent a

considerate amount of time with each other.

Soon enough, they began visiting each other. Dorji's son learnt a lot from Kamzang. A year later, Kamzang agreed to get married to Dorji's son. The two got married in Kamzang's village. It was a grand celebration. A huge crowd had gathered to celebrate the couple's happiness.

It was now time for Kamzang to leave her hometown and set out for her husband's home. And so, Kamzang, along with her husband, Dorji and some other relatives began the long journey back to Thimphu.

On the way, Dorji spotted an abandoned house. The building was dark in colour and the façade looked fragile. It was almost as if the house was swaying with the wind. Dorji said to everyone, "Let's spend the rest of the night in that house."

However, Kamzang immediately resisted.

She said, "No, Father. Let us camp in an open field." Dorji was not fully convinced. But, he did as she said. The group pitched their tents in an open field and called it a day. At night...

GRRR. DHADAM DHOOOOM!

A massive earthquake woke up everyone! They all ran for their lives and waited for the

earthquake to subside. The old, abandoned house crumbled to the ground with the impact of the earthquake. They could see the devastation from afar.

After the earthquake was over, Dorji thanked Kamzang. He said to her, "Daughter, if it hadn't been for you, we would've all been crushed in that house!"

"But how did you know?" asked her husband.

"That house has been abandoned for over a year. Every time I came to Thimphu to

visit you, I noticed that house. No one had tried to improve it. I knew sooner or later that house was going to be swept away in a natural calamity. While I didn't want to take any chances on that front, I also noticed a small hole full of rats. They were all running away. Rats, like most animals, can predict a calamity. Which is why I knew it was best if we spent the night outside in the tents," replied Kamzang.

Dorji smiled and said, "Your quick thinking and knowledge saved all of us. I knew you were the perfect choice for my son and for this family!" They then departed for their home and lived the rest of their lives in happiness and prosperity.

Tamasive the Naughty Monkey

A Story from Bhutan

In the forests of eastern Bhutan, there lived a monkey like no other. He was a mischievous one who would go around nearby villages and harass the residents.

Sometimes he would throw rocks at passers-by, at other times he would enter an animal shed at night and trouble the domesticated animals. Yet another time, he walked into a farmer's house and scattered all his seeds.

This monkey was quite swift and evasive. Every time someone tried to catch him, he would manage to escape through a window or a small opening.

The villagers and farmers were tired of this monkey's antics. They were so used to his naughtiness that they began calling him 'Tamasive', which means 'naughty' in Bhutanese.

While all the villages were aware of this notorious monkey, there was an old couple that lived all alone close to the mountains. The old man was a gullible, innocent farmer. His wife had poor eyesight.

One afternoon, Tamasive was exploring the mountains when he spotted the old man farming. He looked at him and said, "Oh! Looks like I've found my target for today!" He went to the old man and began asking questions.

He said to him, "Good day, Sir. What are you doing?"

"Can't you see, you dumb monkey? I'm planting."

"What are you planting?"

"I'm planting sweet potatoes."

Tamasive thought to himself, "Yummy! I love sweet potatoes. I must find a way to get this old man to cook them for me."

He then continued to bother him by asking him more futile questions.

"How are you planting them?"

"I'm burying them in the ground."

"Why are you planting them?"

"So that I can feed my wife and myself."

"And what will happen then?"

"I will grow some more."

After wearing the old man out, Tamasive thought of a plan. With a smirk on his face, he said to the farmer, "That's not the correct way to plant them, you know?"

The old man replied, "Oh! And what do you know about planting, you stupid monkey?"

"You see," said Tamasive, "I've travelled the depths of this forest and met all kinds of farmers. During my journey, I met one farmer who knew how to grow sweet potatoes so that

they would last an entire year. I just thought you might be interested in acquiring that knowledge. If you don't want it I'll leave..."

The old man thought to himself, "I'm becoming older by the day. If this monkey is actually telling the truth, I'll have to work only for a couple of days in a year and can live the rest of my days in peace."

He said to the monkey, "Friend, please don't

leave. Please teach me how to do it."

Tamasive smiled devilishly and said, "The man who taught me cooked the sweet potatoes and wrapped them in leaves before planting them."

At first, the old man seemed confused but being the gullible man that he was, he chose to believe it. He said, "That's so simple! I must tell my wife!" The old man ran back inside the house to share this wonderful secret with his wife.

However, she was not pleased. She began grumbling and arguing with him. "What rubbish! Don't listen to that monkey!" she shouted.

"Your problem is that you don't listen to anybody!" the old man replied.

"That monkey is taking you for a ride!" his wife warned.

"I am old enough to not be fooled by an animal!"

The couple fought like this for an hour. The old man was adamant and kept arguing. Eventually, he wore his wife down.

She said, "Looks like you've already made up your mind and there's nothing I can do to change it. Fine, I'll cook the sweet potatoes. But if the monkey is lying, I will be very angry."

The old man agreed and his wife started cooking the potatoes.

After an hour, the potatoes were ready. The old lady wrapped them in leaves and gave them to her husband. The old man gave half to Tamasive so he could start planting them too.

However, as soon as Tamasive received his half, he unwrapped the potatoes and began feasting on them.

NOM NOM NOM NOM.

Soon, he had finished all his cooked sweet potatoes. He then proceeded to dig out the sweet potatoes planted by the old man and began eating those too. The poor old man was oblivious of the monkey's evil deeds. Just then, his wife came out of the house to take a look at the progress in the planting. She saw the monkey and shouted...

THIEF!

Tamasive's jig was up. The old man was extremely angry. He began chasing him and said, "I knew I shouldn't have trusted you!"

Tamasive ran into the jungle but the old man followed him there. Tamasive said to himself, "I must quickly climb a tree. The old man won't be

able to catch me."

As he was climbing one of the trees, the old man grabbed his tail and pulled the monkey down aggressively. Tamasive hit his head and started feeling dizzy.

Later, he found himself back at the old man's house. There, the old man tied him up. The couple gave him an angry look. Tamasive started begging them. "Please let me go! I promise I will never trouble you again."

But this time, the old woman was in-charge. She said, "No way, monkey. Haven't you heard the phrase 'Fool me once, shame on you, fool me twice, shame on me'?"

Tamasive was now getting desperate. He said to them, "Okay, ho-ho-how about this? Let me go and I'll work for you."

This gave the old woman a brilliant idea. She said to her husband, "There are mice in the loft that keep eating our grains. We can let this monkey guard it and keep it safe."

And so they did exactly that. The old man locked up the monkey in the loft and said to him, "Keep an eye on our grain and keep it away

from mice. We will feed you once a day."

Finally, the couple was at peace.

The next day, it was awfully quiet in the loft. So, the old woman said to her husband, "Dear, it's strangely quiet up there. I wonder what tricks that monkey is up to. You should probably go and check." And so, the old man climbed into the loft and...

NOOOOOOOOOOOOOOOOO

Tamasive had eaten up all the grains. "Burppppppp," he said. "Kindly excuse me, old man."

The old man had run out of patience. He

grabbed Tamasive and stuffed him in a sack and said, "You wretched monkey! I have had it with you. I'm going to kill you and feed you to the wild animals."

His wife noticed him taking the monkey away and said, "This monkey has brought enough loss to this house. We will kill him and sell him to someone who eats monkey flesh."

"That's a great idea," said the old man. "Let's go

to the spring where we can wash him after killing him." And so, the couple left for the spring near the mountain where they planned to end Tamasive's life once and for all.

Tamasive was extremely worried for his life. He had to put his brain to use. Soon, he came up with a plan.

OOGAAAA OOOOOGAAA AAAA AAAA OOOO!!!

He started making sounds inside the sack and kept moving around. This made it very difficult for the old man to carry him. So, he put the sack down, opened it slightly and said, "What is it that you want, you dull creature?"

Tamasive looked at the couple with innocent eyes and said, "I think my time has come. Eventually, I knew I was going to die. I only have one dying wish. Kill me if you must, but take me down to the river where there is enough water to wash me." The old couple grumbled for a while and then agreed.

After some time, they finally reached the river. It was almost sunset. The old man kept the sack next to a tree and said to his wife, "I am tired. I will rest here for a while."

The old woman decided to go and drink some water from the river. She said to him, "While you're resting, be sure to keep an eye on this

monkey. It's almost sundown and I am not going to be able to see too well."

As soon as the old woman left, Tamasive's head popped out of the sack. He looked around quickly to check if the coast was clear and said to himself, "With that old woman gone, I can easily escape. All I need to do is deal with this old fool."

He sprang out of the sack, teased the old man and made a run for it. The old man began chasing him. "Come here! Today is the day you die."

While running, Tamasive picked up some sand from the ground.

SKREEEEEEEEEEEESSHHH!

Tamasive suddenly halted, looked towards the old man and threw the sand on his face. "Aaaaaaaah! I can't see!" screamed the old man.

His wife followed him with the sack and splashed some water on his eyes. "Quick! He has climbed up this tree. Follow him and push him from there. I will catch him in this sack," she said to him.

The old man climbed up the tree and began looking for Tamasive. "Where are you, little monkey?" said the old man. By now, the sun had completely set. It was dark. The old man was still searching for Tamasive. He knew he had to put an end to this. But, Tamasive shook the branches in such a way that the old man fell straight into the sack.

Since it was dark, the old woman could not differentiate between her husband and the monkey. She took a stick and began thrashing

her husband thinking it was Tamasive. "Die, you little fool," she said.

"Stop, stop, it's me, your husband!" said the old man. The old woman helped him get out of the sack. By then, Tamasive was nowhere to be seen.

The old woman said, "This was all your fault! If only you had listened to me and acted smartly." The old man accepted his mistake and his wife yelled at him all the way home.

As for Tamasive, he realised that Eastern Bhutan had become dangerous for him to live in. So, he was never seen there again.

The Chief and the Glutton

A Story from Nepal

In a small village in a remote part of Nepal, lived a man called Gyanendra with his wife, Maya. Gyanendra was the chief of his village and often had visitors. People would come to him with their problems, and he would have solutions for all of them. He was a man who knew how to get out of tricky situations. On her part, Maya would prepare delicious meals for them and take care of them.

A man named Pampha visited them more often than others. He was a plump man with a thin moustache. He was kind and innocent. He was also overly fond of Maya's cooking. All the other villagers called him a glutton. It was said that Pampha had become friendly with the couple only so that he could visit them and feast at their home.

The couple was surprised to see his endless ability to eat. "I have never seen someone eat so much in my life," said Gyanendra.

"I agree! At this rate, he will finish all the ration in our house. We need to do something about it," said Maya. The couple was in great distress.

The next day, they were awaiting his arrival. This time, Gyanendra had a plan. He told his wife, "He will be here any minute now. I'm going to go out. When he comes, just tell him that we have already eaten and that there is no food at home. That should make him leave immediately." Maya understood his instructions

and patiently waited for Pampha.

Just as they had predicted, Pampha arrived at their doorstep. He said to Maya, "Good evening, Maya! Oh, how hungry I am."

Maya looked at him with a sad face and said, "I'm sorry, my dear friend, but we have already eaten, and I have nothing to offer you. If you're here to see Gyanendra, I'm afraid that he has gone out and won't be available. If he were here, he would've definitely killed a chicken for you."

"Chicken... hmm..." said Pampha. His mouth started salivating at just the thought of it. "I love chicken!" he said to Maya. "It's completely fine if Gyanendra's not here. I shall kill the chicken and you can cook it for me."

NO!

A huge scream came out of Maya. Pampha was startled. "Why not?" he asked her.

Maya didn't know what to say. In a hurry to save face, Maya came up with an instant excuse, "Uhh, you see, you're our guest. I cannot put our guest to work. Gyanendra would get terribly angry."

Pampha laughed and said, "Oh, not at all. How long have I been friends with the two of you? Killing a chicken is no trouble for me."

Pampha asked Maya to keep all the ingredients ready for the meal and walked out of the house to kill the chicken. He was back in less than fifteen minutes. Maya saw him and thought to herself, "I've never seen this man lift a log in his life and look how his hunger drove him to do such a tedious task in such little time."

Maya sat down to prepare the meal. All the while, she had been cursing herself, "Maya, why did you come up with that stupid chicken excuse? Gyanendra is going to be really mad at you."

Just then...

HONEY! I'M HOME! DID HE ---

Gyanendra walked in with an air of confidence. He was certain that Pampha must have left his house by now. To his surprise, Pampha was patiently waiting in the dining room. Gyanendra's face suddenly went pale. "You're back, I've been waiting for you," Pampha said to him.

"Apologies. I had to go out for some important work."

"I know, Maya told me about it! Don't worry. It doesn't matter. Your wife is cooking a delicious meal for me. I can't wait to eat it!"

"Definitely. I'll ask her to hurry up," said Gyanendra and excused himself to go into the kitchen.

Pampha's mouth was watering with anticipation mixed with the aroma of the chicken.

Gyanendra took

Maya inside and began questioning her. "What happened? I thought we had it under control."

"Everything went wrong. He insisted that I cook chicken for him. I did everything I could to stop him but..."

"All right. Let bygones be bygones. Now do as I say. When the chicken is ready, be sure to give him only two pieces. But serve them in the copper bowl that we keep for our guests."

"What about the rest of the chicken?"

"Serve all of it to me in an ordinary clay plate."

And so, Maya did exactly what she was told. She brought the chicken out on two different plates. One in a copper bowl for Pampha, and the other in a clay plate for Gyanendra. While she was setting the table, Gyanendra and Pampha were busy talking.

Gyanendra said to Pampha, "If you don't mind, I will be joining you for dinner. I had eaten before, but I am feeling hungry again."

Pampha replied, "Oh, not at all. Think of this as your house only."

Gyanendra thought to himself, "What a foolish and shameless man. They were about to eat when...

STOP!

Pampha grabbed Gyanendra's wrist that was reaching for the bowl. In an angry tone, he said to him, "What sort of man do you think I am?"

Gyanendra replied, "I don't understand what you mean by that, my friend."

"You are the chief of this village!" said Pampha. "There's no way I'm letting you eat from this clay plate. Give it to me and take the copper plate."

Gyanendra hesitated. He said to Pampha, "No, no! I always eat out of a clay plate at home. Don't worry about that."

But Pampha was persistent. "Absolutely not! I'm not going to take no for an answer." He then proceeded to swap the plates against Gyanendra's wishes.

Gyanendra had to think of a new plan. He thought to himself, "This glutton isn't going

to budge easily. I must do something else."
He signalled to Maya with a wink. Maya understood and waited for his cue.

He then turned to Pampha and said, "As you say, my friend. I'll eat out of the copper plate." But before he started eating, he joined his hands, closed his eyes and began praying loudly.

O EVIL SPIRIT, SPARE US YOUR VISIT TODAY!

O EVIL SPIRIT, SPARE US YOUR VISIT TODAY!

O EVIL SPIRIT, SPARE US YOUR VISIT TODAY!

Pampha was frightened. He gently tapped Gyanendra on the shoulder and said, "What is this evil spirit you're talking about?"

Gyanendra explained to him that the house they lived in was often visited by an evil spirit. It announced its arrival by blowing out the candle. It troubled the couple and left the house only after it was satisfied.

But in reality, there was no evil spirit. This was

yet another plan to get rid of Pampha. Upon hearing the entire story, Pampha said, "Oh, I see. Well, anyway, let's begin eating!"

Just then, Gyanendra signalled Maya from under the table and then...

WOOOOOOOOOOOOOOSH!

Maya softly blew out the candle in the dining room. The room became pitch-black. There was darkness everywhere. "OH NO! The evil spirit is here!" shouted Maya to scare Pampha.

The plan was quite simple. While the lights were out, Gyanendra was going to switch his plate back with Pampha's and continue the meal as planned. But when he went to grab the plate from Pampha...

DISHOOOOOOOOOOM!

Gyanendra felt a strong punch on his face. For a moment he thought perhaps the evil spirit was real. That is when he heard Pampha's voice, "Gyanendra, my friend, are you okay? The evil spirit was trying to steal my chicken but I was too quick for him."

EEEEEEEEEEEEEEEE

Gyanendra let out a small sound of pain as he lay on the ground. Maya ran to fetch some

matchsticks to light the candle.

While she was gone, despite the darkness, Pampha picked up his plate and said, "I wouldn't want the spirit to trouble me anymore. So, if you don't mind, I'll finish my dinner elsewhere. See you tomorrow, my friend." He then left Gyanendra's house.

Meanwhile, Maya came up and lit the candle again. She helped Gyanendra get up. "Get up, are you all right?" she asked him.

"I cannot believe that that glutton can pack a punch," said Gyanendra.

"He has left with both the plates!" replied Maya.

Gyanendra walked into his bedroom with a sense of defeat. Maya tried to console him saying, "Don't worry, dear. We'll outwit him tomorrow."

The Chain of Good Deeds

A Story from Pakistan

Pasha was a young warrior who was kind and compassionate towards all. He was always on the lookout and would carry his sword with him at all times. He was fearless and always up for a challenge.

One day, he was crossing a forest on his horse when...

HISSSSSSSSSSSSSS!!!

KRRRRRRRRRRRRR!!!

He noticed a python and a mongoose fighting each other. They were in a heated battle. The python tried to coil itself around the mongoose but the mongoose was swift enough to escape. He then jumped behind the snake to pinch him with his claws.

While the snake was in a bit of a daze, the mongoose seized the opportunity and began biting the python all over his body. He began to bleed profusely. It was clear that the python was on the defensive, while the mongoose was after his life.

Pasha felt sorry for the python and decided to intervene. He went and told both the animals, "STOP! Please do not fight anymore."

The mongoose pinned the python down and said to Pasha, "Listen, human. Do not come between us. I'm at the point of victory."

As soon as he said that the python tried to sneak away, only to be pinned down again by the mongoose. "Where do you think you're going? The only place you'll be going to now is the afterlife!" said the mongoose to the snake.

This snide behaviour of the mongoose angered Pasha. He drew his sword and...

KHACHAAAAAAAK!

Pasha killed the mongoose. He then looked at the python and said, "Go, you are free now," and began sheathing his sword and getting back on his horse.

The python stopped him and said, "Hold on! You've done me a good turn, and for that...

...YOU MUST DIE!"

As he said that, he quickly coiled himself around Pasha, who was shocked to see this behaviour from an animal he had just rescued.

He said to the python, "I don't get it. I saved your life. You even acknowledged that! Yet you're trying to take my life. Why?"

The python replied, "It's simple. That's the law prevailing here: One who does good to

another invites death upon themself."

"Who made this law? This is outrageous!" said Pasha in panic.

The python then proceeded to tell him a story. "A long time ago, a wealthy man was being pursued by a gang of bandits. They wanted to find the secret hideout where he stashed all his wealth. The man was desperately looking for a place to hide.

"After running for a while, the man found a clump of trees. He rushed to the middle of the grove and began praying, 'Hide me, O Trees, or I am doomed.' The trees felt pity for him and bent their branches to hide the man from the bandits' line of sight.

"When they arrived at the spot, the bandits searched for him for several hours before finally giving up and leaving. Thus, the trees saved his life!

"'Thank you so much! I owe you my life! I've never seen trees like you before. You're so strong.'

The wealthy man kept showering praises on the trees. He was extremely grateful."

Pasha interrupted the python and said, "LOOK AT THAT MAN! You just said he was grateful, unlike YOU!"

The python hissed at Pasha and said, "SSSSSHUT UP! I'VE NOT FINISHED." He continued the story...

"However, a few days later, the wealthy man sent three men to the same place. They identified the trees as per the wealthy man's description. They picked up axes and got to work.

TAK TAK TAK TAK TAK TAK!

"And just like that, they cut down the trees. The wealthy man thought that the trees that saved him from his enemies would make for great material for a house that he was building for himself.

"The man had returned evil for good, and it brought a change in the entire jungle. From that day onwards, all of us here have been doing exactly what the man did...

RETURNING EVIL FOR GOOD."

The python then tightened his grip and said, "And for those reasons, I will have to eat you."

Pasha looked at him and said, "I didn't know that such a law really exists here..."

The python replied, "I don't care whether you know or not. Prepare to die!"

Pasha begged the python to let him go. He said to him, "Please, you have to believe me!

I was only crossing this jungle to fetch my wife, Mira, from her mother's place. How about this? Allow me to go and fetch her. You can eat me on my return journey. At least, that way she will know what happened to me."

The python obliged. "That's understandable. But beware! If you try to trick me..."

Pasha interrupted him and said, "I won't! You have my word. I shall return by this same route and deliver myself to you within seven days." And so, Pasha bought some time for himself.

Pasha reached his mother-in-law's place to fetch Mira. He did not tell anybody about his encounter with the snake. However, there was an air of tension on his face. He spent some time there and in a couple of days decided to go back home with his wife.

On the return journey, Mira travelled in a chariot along with another driver. She noticed Pasha's peculiar behaviour. She thought to herself, "Pasha has not been himself since the last couple of days. He looks frightened. Is he expecting some danger in the forest? I wish he would confide in me."

When they reached the forest, Pasha told the driver to take his horse and go back home. From thereon, he drove the chariot.

"Why did you send him away?" asked Mira.

"You will soon know," Pasha replied.

"No, please tell me now! I am your wife. It is my right to know."

"You are right. It started when I was coming to get you..."

And so, Pasha began narrating the entire incident to Mira. He was almost done talking when the two of them encountered the snake.

HISSSSSSSSSSSSSSS!

"There he is! That's him," said Pasha as he pointed towards the python.

"I have resssspect for you, Pasha. You are a man of your word," said the Python. There was anticipation in his eyes.

Pasha got down from the horse, looked at Mira and with a very heavy voice said, "My beloved Mira, this is the end. It's all over for me. Please take care of yourself."

Mira was almost in tears. She said to him, "No! There's got to be another way!"

She got down from the chariot and kneeled before the python and begged, "Please, spare him! I beg you!"

But the python did not care. He replied, "I'm sorry but there's nothing that I can do. I have to uphold the law. Besides, I'm starving!"

Mira began reasoning with the python. She said to him, "If you eat him then I will be left without support. While I understand my husband has breached the law of this forest and must be punished for the same, what have I done to be punished? I have broken no law whatsoever." The python did not have any answer to that. He asked the couple to wait at the same spot while he went to a nearby cave.

When the python returned, he had a ball of manure in his mouth. He placed it near Mira's feet and said to her, "Take it. It's a magical ball. Throw it into your field at home, and you will get a bountiful harvest, year after year. You will live a prosperous life and won't need your husband to support you. I have no use for this ball anyway."

Mira took the ball and said, "Thank you. But you must understand that prosperity will make my neighbours envious. Who will protect me from my enemies?"

The python was losing his calm. He looked at her and said, "O woman! You are testing my patience! Wait here." He went back to his cave.

He returned with a ball of mud. He gave it to her and said, "Keep this. This too is magical. Throw it at whoever annoys, threatens or insults you. They will instantly turn into ash. It'll give you all the protection you'll ever need."

Mira was extremely happy with this gesture. Pasha was unsure what was going on. She said to the python, "This will be very useful for me. Thank you so much. I am overwhelmed by your kindness. And since you've done me a good turn, that means...

YOU MUST DIE!"

The python was terrified! He had been bested by Mira. There was a sudden change in his tone. He said to her, "No, no! Please do not throw that at me! I'll do whatever you want. Please spare me."

Mira said, "Spare my husband and I'll let you go." The python had no other choice but to give up. The terrified python fled into the depths of the forest.

Meanwhile, Mira picked up the two balls and fled home with Pasha.

Half Knowledge

A Story from Bhutan

Prince Jigme and Loden were childhood friends. At a very young age, Jigme's father sent him to a monastery in the mountains of Bhutan. He wanted him to learn how to be a man so that when he came of age, he could be a worthy successor. The Abbot there was well revered and knowledgeable.

The King wanted someone to accompany Prince Jigme. Loden gladly agreed to go along.

The two boys spent years learning life skills at the monastery. They learned a range of things, such as archery, how to talk to animals, morality, compassion and quick-wittedness, and built their overall mental and physical strength. The Abbot never discriminated between the two of them and treated them as equals.

After twelve years, they had finally learnt everything from the Abbot. He called the two of them and said to Prince Jigme, "You have completed twelve years here, Prince Jigme, and we have taught you all we could. You know everything there is to know about the arts, sciences, weapons and even the language of animals. Now, you can go back home an educated man."

Prince Jigme was happy to hear this. "What about me, master?" asked Loden, expecting a similar response.

The Abbot said to Loden, "You, Loden, will have to stay another year! Your studies are not over yet."

WHAT!

Loden could not believe his ears. He thought to himself, "How can he even say that? Prince Jigme and I were taught by the same tutors at the same time. I know as much as he does!" He tried to reason with Abbot, "I think I have learnt

enough, revered Sir. My duty is to accompany the prince. Please permit me to go home with him."

The Abbot responded, "It looks like you have made up your mind. Very well then, as you wish. But I must warn you that half knowledge is dangerous. My advice to you would be that you complete your education." However, Loden did not pay heed to the Abbot's words.

The next morning, the two young men set out for home. After riding for a couple of hours, they reached an abandoned valley.

Loden said to Prince Jigme, "My throat is parched. We need to find water. This is a dry, waterless place." Just then...

SWOOOOOOOOP!

A crow started circling around the two of them. He began cawing...

KOOOO-AAAAAAY!
KOOOO-AAAAAAY!
KOOOO-AAAAAAY!

Prince Jigme looked at the crow, nodded and said, "He says there's water under one of the rocks." The Prince dismounted and began kicking the rocks around. After a couple of minutes, the Prince declared, "Aha! Found it!" There was a small pool of water under one of the rocks.

The two of them drank the water and refreshed themselves. Loden thought to himself, "I thought that the crow

was just screeching. How did Prince Jigme understand his language? Could it be that he really knows more than I do?"

After resting for a while, they resumed their journey. However, the thought of the Prince

being smarter than him was still lurking in Loden's mind. He kept thinking, "I don't want people back home to think that even though we both trained at the same place, at the same time, the Prince knows more than me. It'll be humiliating. Everyone will think I'm a duffer!"

Several hours passed. Prince Jigme wanted to rest. He found a cosy spot and said, "It's nice and shady. Let's set up camp here for the night." He found a tree and made himself comfortable under it. Meanwhile, Loden decided to hunt for some food.

He ventured deep into the forest. He found a tree with some ripe and juicy berries. As he was picking them, a sparrow came near him and began chirping.

CHIRRUP! CHIRRUP!

Loden listened to it carefully and said, "So, you're saying that they're

poisonous? Understood! Thanks for the warning." As he was returning, he couldn't help but wonder, "I was able to understand the sparrow but not the crow. Perhaps, my knowledge is indeed imperfect."

By now, jealousy had clouded his judgement. He thought, "I can't have anyone more knowledgeable than me at the palace, even if it is the King's son! I'll have to do something about it." He began formulating devious plans.

He went back with the berries and offered them to the Prince. Prince Jigme began eating them and soon fell unconscious. "Aha! He's finally dead!" said Loden to himself. He then set off for the palace, alone.

The berries were not as poisonous as Loden's mind. Even after killing his friend, he kept thinking ill of him. He thought to himself, "All this knowledge and yet he wasn't able to save himself. Now, not only will I become the most knowledgeable man at the palace but also the most qualified to be the next king!"

He now began to think of a way to justify his friend's death. He thought, "I'll tell the King that we had a race to see who would reach the palace first and that I have no idea what happened to him after that. I will then lead a search party and after pretending to search for him, I will declare him deceased."

Just then...

KO-KOW KO-KOW KO-KOW!

The crow had returned to tell Loden something. He heard the crow and said, "If I got that right, he's saying there are hungry butterflies ahead. It could be that the vegetation over there has dried up and now

there's no food for them. Well, best of luck to them." And he proceeded to take that path.

Meanwhile, back at the tree, Prince Jigme had woken up and was not really dead!

He thought to himself, "Wow! It feels like I have slept for a thousand years. I wonder where Loden is. I hope he is all right. I must look for him."

After exploring the area, looking for Loden, Prince

Jigme came across the tree with the same berries that he had eaten earlier. As he was examining them, the sparrow returned.

CHIRRUP!
CHIRRUP!
CHIRRUP!

"What?" exclaimed Prince Jigme. "These berries will put me into deep slumber? No wonder I slept so soundly. Loden must've thought that I became unconscious and went to get help."

Just then, the crow came with some terrible news.

KO-KOW KO-KOW KO-KOW!

"What?" said Prince Jigme. "There's a hungry tiger ahead and my friend has taken the same path? Thanks for the warning, friend. I must go and save him."

Prince Jigme hurried to look for his friend. Soon, he found the footprints of Loden's horse and began following that path. A short distance ahead, he found Loden's horse. The horse was startled. Prince Jigme quickly calmed it down and took the horse along with him.

LOOOOOODEEEEEEEEEEEEN!

Prince Jigme soon saw Loden. He was cornered by a tiger. "Friend, help me!" cried Loden. This further agitated the tiger.

RAAAAAAAWRRRR!

Loden was helpless. He did not have his bow and arrow with him nor any other weapon to help him defend himself. Prince Jigme knew that he had to do something quickly. He drew an arrow from his quiver, took a proper stance and just as the tiger was about to pounce on Loden, he shot it.

ZZTAACCCCCK!

The tiger was a bit shaken. He turned around to see the Prince and decided to attack him. But Prince Jigme used his horse to gain the upper hand against the tiger. He quickly dismounted and drew his sword to pounce on the tiger.

The two of them got into a heated battle and eventually Prince Jigme managed to make the tiger flee. He then went to pick up his friend, who had fallen on the ground.

"Are you all right, Loden?" he asked him.

"Yes. My horse threw me at the sight of the tiger and bolted."

"Don't you worry. Everything's fine now. I found your horse. Let's go home."

Once he was out of shock, Loden began thinking, "He's so skilled and noble. He was able to control his horse with ease and even calm mine down. His weaponry skills were also superior. When I saw the tiger, I completely froze. I even misunderstood the crow, and led both of us to our deaths. I'm driven by jealousy, pride and selfishness. I'm just glad that the berries did not harm him."

Once they were ready to be on their way, Loden said to Prince Jigme, "Friend, you go back to the palace. I'm going back to the monastery. I've still got a lot to learn. Horse-riding, weaponry, talking to birds and more importantly how to become a better human being."

Prince Jigme shook his hand and said to him, "Very well then, friend. I'll miss you. Come back soon."

And so, the two young men rode away in opposite directions. Loden went back to the monastery to complete his education. Meanwhile, Prince Jigme went back to the palace to embrace the next stage of his life – mastering statecraft!

FASCINATING FOLKTALES FROM INDIA

WRITTEN BY

RITUJA SAWANT

A Santhal Tale of Creation

A Folktale from Odisha

"In the beginning, the world was not as we know it today. There was only water everywhere. And the world was concealed under these primordial waters... deep, blue-black and mysterious..."

In a classroom in a small village in Mayurbhanj, chaos broke out. Everyone started to speak at once.

"Only water... how can that be?"

"Did humans also breathe under water?"

"Deep and blue-black? Sounds cold and scary..."

"How did the water hide the whole world?"

"What's primordial?"

The storyteller raised both his hands asking the students to sit down and replied, "All right, all right... settle down. Let's listen to the story and see if it answers all your questions."

Every week, the school had a special storytelling session, where an elderly person from the village would come and share captivating folk stories from their tribe. These stories had travelled down from one generation to the next; through the oral tradition of storytelling, often told during festivals around a bonfire. The ancient tales were narrated in a sing-song way, their rhythmic words often repeated as a chorus.

Today's storyteller was a wise old gentleman

from the Santhal tribe who was eager to share the fascinating tale of creation, a version retold specially by his tribe of Mayurbhanj, Odisha. The Santhal tribe is the largest tribal population in South Asia and they mostly live in the states of Odisha, West Bengal, Jharkhand and Bihar.

The storyteller stood in the centre of the classroom, all eyes were on him and continued...

As I was saying, in ancient times, the world as we know it, was surrounded by deep dark waters.

As 'Thakur Baba', the supreme being of the Santhal tribe, watched the churning and chaos of the oceans, he wondered to himself, "Hmm... these waters are simply magnificent... but they are hiding a whole world within... How do I begin the process of creation?"

He pondered on how to raise the earth out of the water as he wanted to create many

different forms of life, including the first people.

It was in deep meditation that the answer came to him. "Of course! I must seek the help of Lita Gadet!"

And so, the divine Thakur Baba summoned his most ardent follower. Lita Gadet is a god-sage in the Santhal culture, similar to Narada, considered the son of Brahma in Hindu tradition. It is believed that Lita Gadet could walk around the universe in a mere two and a half steps in the blink of an eye!

As Lita Gadet appeared in front of his beloved deity, he bowed his head in reverence. "My lord! I came as soon as I received your summons. How can I be of service to you?"

Thakur Baba was pleased to meet his most dedicated devotee and raised his hand in blessing. "My dear Lita, I have a special task for you. Are you up for a challenge?"

"Speak, O Great One! Your wish is my command!"

"The earth is submerged under water. We need to find a way to bring it out of the deep waters."

Lita Gadet thought momentarily and then his face lit up. "I think I may have a solution, my dear lord. What if we could find someone strong

enough in the waters to lift out the earth?"

"That is a good idea. But who can we ask?"

"Thakur Baba, there are many good options. There is the turtle, the Balia fish, the crocodile and many more. We have only to ask for their help and we shall receive it."

And so, Lita sat down with his eyes closed. He took a deep breath and started with a series of invocations and chants. He first sang an invocation to the ancient Hindu deity Indra and then the other gods.

"... All you creatures who live in these deep, mysterious waters, please come out. We need your help!"

The mighty turtle was the first to arrive. There was a loud splash as the enormous turtle with a leather-like shell emerged from the waters. He lifted his dark-grey head above the surface, and looked up at Lita and said, "Greetings, dear Lita! What can I do for you?"

"O mighty turtle, we need your help to raise the earth from Patala – the bottom of the sea – on

your strong back."

The mighty turtle considered the task and hesitated. "But if I carry the whole earth on my back, how will I eat? All my attention will be on balancing the earth. I will have to fast forever. I will go hungry. No, no, that simply cannot do!"

Thakur Baba considered the turtle's plight and offered, "Do not fret! All the offerings made to the gods all over the world will come right into your mouth. You will never go hungry. In fact, you will live well and forever!"

Just as he said this, many other powerful sea creatures also arrived. Lita looked at these glorious creatures and suggested, "Baba, here we not only have the turtle, but also the Balia fish, the crocodile, the crab, the prawn and the earthworm. Maybe they can all give it a shot and try to get the earth out of the waters."

"That seems fair..." agreed Thakur Baba.

So, the gigantic, sturdy crab went first. He

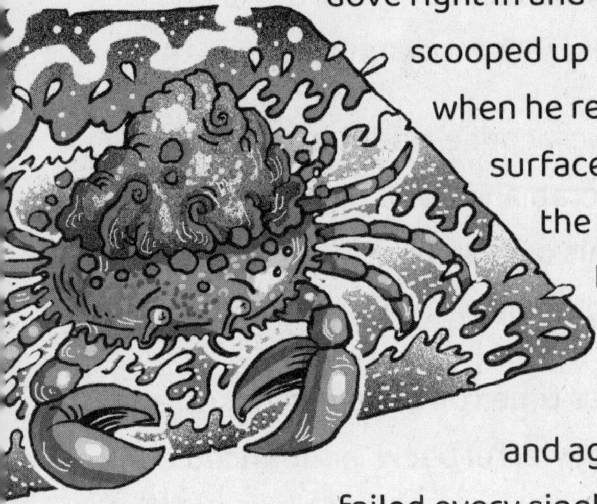

dove right in and victoriously scooped up the earth. But when he reached the surface of the sea, the earth had all but washed away. He tried again and again, but failed every single time.

Next was the turn of the Balia fish. Brave and nimble, she swiftly swam down and up with the earth in her mouth. But the earth was far too heavy and more than a mouthful for her. Unfortunately, in her attempt to lift the earth, her mouth tore at the sides. The great Thakur Baba kindly

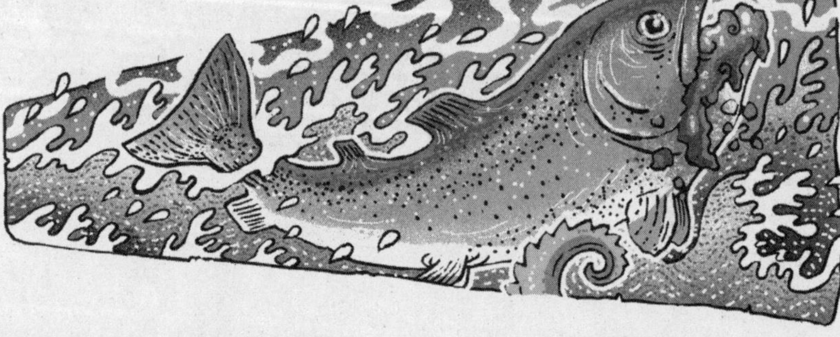

stitchedup the sides of her mouth. Having been unsuccessful, she swam away.

The ferocious crocodile, undeterred by the failure of the crab and the Balia fish, was confident of his own abilities. He was, after all, a tough and mighty being of the ancient waters.

"Move aside. It's time for the earth to surface riding on my powerful back!" announced the crocodile as he disappeared into the deep blue waters.

But when he returned, the earth had once again washed away. The crocodile tried a few times,

but finally gave up, exhausted. He left quietly, his pride hurt and feeling a little humbled.

Then came the prawn, with a large head and a swinging tail. His best efforts were no match for the mighty earth. He nearly got smashed under the mound on his first attempt.

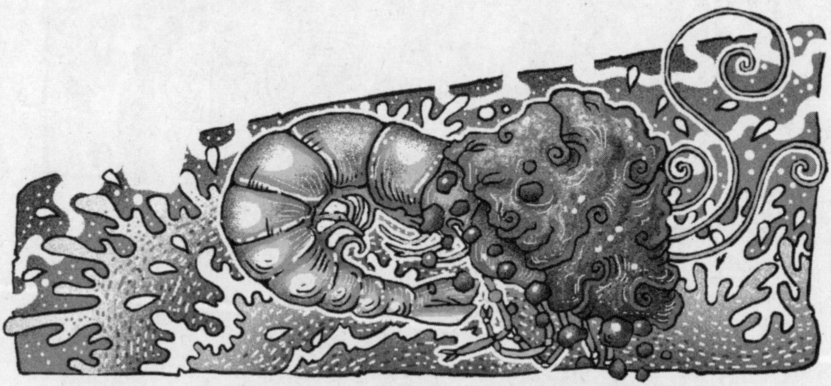

And now, it was the frail earthworm's turn. He had a bright idea. "I have a plan which I can execute with the mighty turtle's help," he suggested humbly. "I will bind a pole from the depths of the ocean to the surface. I will suck up the earth and deposit it on the turtle's back."

The turtle agreed to work with the earthworm. And so, they started.

The earthworm kept piling up the earth from the bottom of the sea, little by little, on top of the turtle's strong shell.

But as they progressed, the mound of earth on the turtle's back got bigger and bigger, and the turtle became more and more tired.

He trembled and wobbled and cried, "Stop! I cannot go on much longer. The earth is too heavy for me. I cannot hold it in place anymore!"

CRASH! SPLASH!

The earth slipped off the turtle's back and fell back into the sea. The turtle scuttled away. But Lita Gadet was not one to give up. He chased after the turtle and brought him back.

"Tie him up with an iron chain so that he is firm and unable to move," ordered Thakur Baba.

Too tired to protest, the turtle gave in. The earthworm got started all over again and only stopped after he had collected the last bit of earth from Patala.

Thakur Baba and Lita Gadet admired his perseverance and applauded the earthworm's effort. He took their blessings and thanked the mighty turtle as he left.

The mission was finally accomplished, with the earth out of the waters, safely held in place on the turtle's back.

And that's how the earth came to be...

The Santhali storyteller smiled, paused and looked at the sea of eager faces. The curious students, of course, had even more questions this time, which he answered patiently.

"But who could have levelled the earth?" asked a young girl.

"Well, some say it was ploughed and the furrows became the plains, and the mounds became the mountains."

"And what about humans? How could they live on this unstable earth?" asked another student.

"Ah! Excellent question! In fact, this was the question that Lita Gadet posed to the mighty Thakur Baba. And within seconds, Lita himself came up with an ingenuous solution!" said the storyteller and continued...

Lita informed Thakur Baba that in the heavens, where the gods lived, a pristine dove had laid eggs in a nest made of the Dooba grass. She had brought it from another heaven and planted it there, which had made her nest stable and strong. The same could also be used for the earth. So, Lita Gadet brought some of the amazing Dooba grass and planted it on the earth. It grew rapidly like magic and soon its long roots held the earth firmly in place, making it stable for humans to live.

As the storyteller finished telling this wondrous Santhal tale of creation, the students could hear the drummers come in. They rushed out into the yard. The school had organised a special surprise to celebrate the Santhal festival of Baha Parab in the traditional way.

'Baha' means flower and this festival takes place in spring. The people of the Santhal tribe dance to the rhythmic beats of the Madal drums and everyone cheerfully participates in this joyous tradition.

After an evening of dance and music, the students grew tired. As they rested their heads that night, they went to sleep full of thoughts of crabs, crocodiles, earthworms, turtles, and the Santhal story of creation.

THE WISE FOUR

A Folktale from Maharashtra

You'll be born in the greatest kingdom,
Sweet little one, it's time to rest,
Dream of kindness and wisdom,
Be like Veerasena as he's the best!

This and many such lullabies were often sung by expectant mothers in honour of their great King Veerasena. Under his reign, the kingdom was peaceful and prosperous and its people happy.

Born to the brave King Shurasena, Veerasena was a kind and generous prince. Even as a child, he had always been caring and giving towards young and old, rich and poor, alike. His plentiful acts of kindness had not only won the hearts of the people of his own kingdom, but also gotten him the admiration of the neighbouring kingdoms.

The long-awaited day arrived when the popular prince was crowned king. His subjects cheered and welcomed the new reign with open arms and festivities. From a splendid procession to a royal feast, and from booming drums to cheerful dancing, the grand celebrations lasted a whole week. Such was the charm and glory of King Veerasena!

While kindness came naturally to King Veerasena, for wisdom and guidance he depended on his four wise ministers. They were sensible, honest, fair and, most importantly, they cared deeply for the good of the people

of their kingdom. This made the 'Wise Four' – Ramabai, Pushpatai, Sitaram and Adinath – a great team and the king could always count on their support.

Every morning, they pored over the problems faced by the people and advised King Veerasena with suitable solutions.

"Your Majesty, the rains have been wreaking havoc for a few days now. We must prepare just in case the river overflows and there are floods," said Ramabai, looking worried.

"That's good thinking. Let's stock up the granary with food and water at the earliest," ordered King Veerasena.

"Very well, Your Majesty. It shall be arranged," replied Adinath dutifully.

Every day, there were small and big problems which King Veerasena tackled with ease with the help of his trusted ministers.

As was the custom, King Veerasena would regularly go on tours to fulfil his royal duties and accept invitations from friendly neighbouring kingdoms.

One day, when he had just returned from one such royal tour, King Veerasena was lost deep in thought.

He gathered his four ministers and made a strange announcement, "I have decided that I want to live in the most lavish and spectacular palace in all the lands!"

"Your Majesty, with all due respect, I request you to reconsider. We should definitely build a beautiful and comfortable palace, but within our means. That would be a sensible thing to do," suggested Pushpatai gently. She did not want to dampen the young king's enthusiasm.

"I agree with Pushpatai, Sire. After all, our kingdom is not as wealthy as some of the other rulers around us," added Sitaram.

"A king's palace is symbolic of his status and the might of his kingdom. A lavish palace would clearly send out the message that not only are our people comfortable and wealthy, they also believe in spending on the good things in life," stated King Veerasena in no uncertain terms.

"But, Your Majesty, the royal treasury at the moment does not have enough to build such an expensive palace!" exclaimed Ramabai.

But King Veerasena was adamant. "There's a simple solution. We will collect a special tax from all the citizens to gather enough money to cover the cost of the new palace."

Ramabai, Pushpatai, Sitaram and Adinath were speechless. In all their years of being loyal ministers of the kingdom, they had not heard of a more foolish or wasteful idea. They explained how the wealth of the people needs to be used wisely for their benefit and how

it is the king's duty to improve the life of the citizens, not the other way round. They tried very hard to talk some sense into their king, but he would have none of it. His mind was made up and his patience was wearing thin. He was furious with the Wise Four!

"If the ministers of this kingdom don't follow their king's commands and don't have his best interests at heart, they have no purpose to serve here. I order all four of you to leave my kingdom immediately. You are banished!" King Veerasena fumed.

Disappointed and shocked, the four ministers did as they were told. They carried their humble belongings and left.

"What has come over our beloved king! He was never like this," groaned Adinath.

"Let's pray and hope that he realises his mistake and changes his mind about the palace," said Sitaram, as they exited the palace gates.

With nowhere to go, the four banished ministers walked aimlessly till the noon sun was high. They had been walking through the fields all morning. Tired and thirsty, they decided to rest a little before they moved on.

They found a gigantic, old banyan tree and took shelter in its soothing shade. While Sitaram wiped his forehead and Pushpatai quenched her thirst, Adinath stared gloomily into the distance.

Meanwhile, Ramabai was looking intently at something and said, "Don't look so sad, dear Adinath. I have an idea. Let's play a fun game. Come, look at these footprints in the mud. What do you think?"

"It's obvious that they belong to a camel," said Sitaram.

"Yes, yes, a camel, of course. But that's not the game. It will be fun if we can all try to guess some things about this camel, merely from

his footprints," challenged Ramabai, grinning.

Adinath, Pushpatai and Sitaram agreed that it sounded like fun and decided to play along.

Just then, a very hassled young man passed by the banyan tree, muttering to himself. "Oh no, no, no... not again... this time I think she is lost forever! How could I have been so careless!"

The Wise Four noticed his hurried walk and worried frown. They called out to him, "Who are you? What's the matter?"

"Huh!" he noticed them suddenly and cried, "I am Raghu and my camel is missing!"

On hearing the mention of a camel, all four ministers stood up and started asking questions.

"Ah! A camel, is it? By any chance was she lame in one of her hind legs?" asked Sitaram eagerly.

"Yes, yes, she was! She was attacked by a wolf a few months ago! Which way did she go? Please tell me," said Raghu, looking hopeful.

"First tell me, my dear. Was your camel also blind in one eye?" questioned Pushpatai.

"Yes! In fact, she once walked right into a tree and unfortunately that's how she hurt her eye! Can you please point me in her direction?"

But instead of an answer, all Raghu got was yet another question, this time from Ramabai, "We don't know where she went. But can you tell us about her tail? Would it be correct to say she does not have one?"

"That is correct! She lost her tail in an accident last month when a cart ran over it! Why won't you just tell me where she is?" yelled Raghu, frustrated.

"We would love to help you. But we haven't actually seen your camel, who, if I may say so, is also quite ill. Isn't she?" added Adinath, as kindly as he could.

But Raghu was now furious and convinced that the four strangers were trying to trick him.

"That's it! I know what's going on here. You all aren't telling me where she is because you stole her, you crooks! Where have you hidden her?"

"No, no... Raghu... listen... don't misunderstand... we really haven't even seen her... please believe us..." tried Ramabai.

But Raghu just pointed an angry finger at them and accused the four wise ministers, "You four stole her! I just know it! How else could you possibly know so much about my camel without ever seeing her?"

Adinath and Sitaram tried to pacify Raghu, but he would not listen.

"Give me back my camel right now," he demanded. "Or I will take this theft to King Veerasena!"

"There is nothing we can do as we did not take your camel," the four ministers said together.

Raghu stomped off muttering, "I will get justice and I will get my camel back! Just wait and watch, you crooks! I will be right back!"

Luckily for Raghu, he did not have to go very far. King Veerasena was on his evening rounds and Raghu ran into him.

Raghu told King Veerasena the whole story and pleaded for justice, "Your Majesty, only you can help a poor and wronged man like me. All I ever had was my camel and now that has also been taken from me. I have nothing... absolutely nothing."

The king heard Raghu patiently and assured him that justice would be served. He asked Raghu to take him to the people who he believed had stolen his precious camel.

Soon, the king and his soldiers led by Raghu arrived at the gigantic banyan tree.

"There they are, Sire! The four crooks! And

look, they are still standing around. Not even afraid of the mighty King Veerasena himself!" chided Raghu.

King Veerasena recognised his ministers. He knew that they could never steal from anyone. He decided to investigate and find out the truth of the theft. He gave the ministers a fair chance to explain their side of the story. That was what the Wise Four had always advised the king to do.

King Veerasena questioned them one by one. But they claimed to be innocent and simply told the king that they had never set eyes on Raghu's camel.

"How could we steal something we haven't even seen, Your Majesty?" pleaded Adinath.

"You liar! How dare you lie straight to the king's face! Have you no shame?" yelled Raghu.

King Veerasena asked everyone to calm down and asked his banished ministers, "This man says that you identified his camel correctly to every last detail. Now, how did you know that it was lame in one hind leg?"

Sitaram promptly explained, "From her footprints, Your Majesty! Please take a look at these prints in the mud. As you can see, she wasn't able to place her injured leg firmly on the ground. However, we can clearly see the other three footprints, which are much deeper."

"Hmm... that makes sense," said King Veerasena looking at Raghu.

"That may be

so, Your Majesty," said Raghu warily. "But how could they possibly know that she could only see with one eye?"

"I will explain," offered Pushpatai. "The poor camel can only see from her right eye." Pushpatai pointed to the path they were standing on and continued, "If you notice, the grass on the right side of this path has been

eaten by Raghu's camel. But the grass on the left side of the path is untouched."

Intrigued, King Veerasena got off his horse and personally inspected the grass.

"Hmm... that seems fair. What do you think?" he said looking at Raghu.

Raghu agreed and said, "Sure, that is a good point. But what about her missing tail? Not like it would leave a trail or eat grass. How did they guess that my camel has no tail?"

"Oh, that was plain and clear due to these gnats! Look at them, right here," said Ramabai, as she kneeled to a gnat-filled spot on the path.

"These dead gnats? Am I to believe that the gnats told you about the camel's missing tail! They are not even alive! Ha-ha!" mocked Raghu.

But Ramabai was not rattled. She smiled and spoke directly to Raghu, "My dear man, the gnats are alive. They are just too full to move."

"WHAT?" Even King Veerasena was surprised and looked more closely.

"The gnats cannot fly as they've had so much blood to drink... the poor camel's blood. And that wouldn't have happened if she had a tail to swat them away," explained Ramabai triumphantly.

"That is impressive!" applauded King Veerasena.

The reasons and explanations shared by the four ministers were so brilliant that this time even Raghu agreed that they could not have stolen his missing camel.

"They are just very clever and wise. I take back my complaint."

King Veerasena was happy to hear that the matter was resolved and generously offered that his soldiers would help Raghu find his missing camel. Raghu thanked the king for his kind gesture and walked away with a bunch of soldiers in search of his camel.

King Veerasena then turned to the Wise Four and realised his folly. He knew that their wisdom and honesty were invaluable to his kingdom and their people.

King Veerasena was nothing if not humble. He requested his trusted ministers to join back immediately.

"We serve at the pleasure of the king," they all said in agreement.

But the king had one last question, "Tell me, how did you know that the camel was ill?"

"By looking at the dung, Your Majesty. It is not the same as that of a healthy camel," said Adinath smugly.

"Ha-ha! That is very wise. Very wise indeed. But I must admit that I have figured out that actually I am the wisest of us all... because I have surrounded myself with the wisest people in the world!"

King Veerasena and the Wise Four headed back happily to the palace. The four ministers continued to serve the kingdom wisely for many many years to come.

They kept King Veerasena from making any wrong decisions in the future...

... except maybe a few because even a king is allowed a mistake or two.

Pearls of Kindness

A Folktale from Kumaon

In the foothills of the Himalayas, there was an enchanting village on the outskirts of Bageshwar in Kumaon. Here, the skies were a bright blue, the fields lush green and stream waters always sweet. The villagers lived merrily in this paradise of beauty and quiet peace.

Jaidutt was born in this charming village and had grown up admiring the spectacular mountains surrounded by dense forests full of

oak, deodar and pine trees. He loved his town so much that he had chosen to be a tour guide and spend all his life proudly showing around scores of eager travellers. Bageshwar was known for its scenic rivers, icy blue glaciers and its famed temples. People came from all over Uttarakhand and the rest of the country to soak in this scenic beauty.

Every morning, Jaidutt would begin his day with a dip in the pristine waters of the Sarayu river. This had been his ritual ever since he could remember and, over the years, he had taught his sons to do the same.

Now in his later years, Jaidutt lived by himself in his humble family home on top of a small hill. His sons were married and had families of their own. His two sons worked in the faraway town of Pithoragarh. But their wives continued to live in the village in separate houses, comfortably settled with their children.

After his beloved wife's passing, Jaidutt had learnt to manage his home on his own. He cooked his meals, cleaned the house and even washed his own clothes. Of late, he was feeling more and more tired, but he was too proud to ask anyone for help.

One morning, the sky was lighting up with the first rays of the sun and the magnificent Himalayas were glimmering in the distance. Jaidutt, an early riser, started walking down to the river for his bath, when he almost slipped. Luckily, he was able to stop his fall with the walking stick, else he would have had a bad tumble downhill.

Jaidutt realised he was getting too old to care for all his needs on his own and decided to ask for help.

"Hmmm... what if I ask one of my daughters-in-law for help? Maybe one of them could just bring me the water of Sarayu daily," he thought to himself.

He decided to go for one last dip in the sacred Sarayu and on his way back he stopped by his elder daughter-in-law Paruli's home.

His elder son Manoj and Paruli had done well for themselves. They had bought a big, spacious village house along with a large piece of adjoining land for farming. While Manoj was away working in Pithoragarh, Paruli looked after their home, farm and children.

When Jaidutt reached their front yard, he called out to Paruli, "Buari! O Buari! Please come out. This is Saurju."

'Buari' and 'Saurju' is the Kumaoni way of addressing the daughter-in-law and father-in-law, respectively. Even though Paruli was blessed with material wealth, she was not the most generous person. In fact, she was ill-tempered, selfish and wore a perpetual frown.

When she came out into the front yard, she barely even greeted her father-in-law with a smile.

"Buari, it is so good to see you. Are the children at school?" Jaidutt enquired.

She replied irritably, "Yes, they are! Do you need something?"

"Actually, I have been finding it very difficult to walk down to the Sarayu river for my bath. Since you go down to the river every morning, I was wondering if you could fetch me one small bucket of water daily," Jaidutt requested.

Paruli responded quickly. "Me? Oh Saurju, you know me, I would if I could. But I have got such a large land to till that I hardly get any time. Why don't you ask Hansu? I am sure she can easily spare some time. After all, she has a very small field compared to mine."

Jaidutt was disappointed but he waved goodbye to her and decided to pay a visit to his younger daughter-in-law. The path leading up to Hansu's house was uneven and Jaidutt walked cautiously with the help of his sturdy walking stick.

When he reached her front door, Hansu was busy patting cowdung cakes on her outer wall. Hansu's home was a humble one and the cowdung cakes were used as fuel to light up the chulha or domestic stove for cooking.

As soon as she saw her father-in-law, Hansu welcomed him into her home. Jaidutt sat down. Hansu washed her hands and offered him a hot cup of tea.

Jaidutt had been walking all morning and Hansu's tea turned out to be a refreshing delight. While Hansu was not as rich as Paruli, she was kind and caring towards one and all.

When Jaidutt repeated his request to his

younger daughter-in-law, she immediately agreed to help. "Just a bucket of water? Of course, I will fetch it for you, Saurju. It would be my pleasure. Is there anything else you need?"

"Oh Buari! Bless your kind soul. May you live a long and happy life. I will always pray to Gollu Dev for your health and prosperity!" he replied gratefully.

Hansu smiled and waved, as Jaidutt slowly walked back home.

So, from the next day onwards, every morning, Hansu turned up at the break of dawn at Jaidutt's house with a bucket full of sacred

Sarayu water. Not just that, when she noticed that the yard and the house could do with a thorough cleaning, she decided to do that as well.

In a few days, she began cleaning the house and making breakfast for her ageing father-in-law while he finished his bath. She also offered to wash his dhoti at the village naula, a freshwater spring, nearby. She would then hang it to dry in Jaidutt's yard and take his leave for the day.

Days turned into weeks and weeks into months. Hansu kept her word and every morning, like clockwork, she would come by to help Jaidutt.

One day, as she was washing Jaidutt's dhoti, something rather strange happened. As she was rinsing it, the water droplets started bouncing up and down. They also looked rather large and shiny. When Hansu bent down to take a closer look, she was stunned to discover that they were shiny white pearls!

"Pearls! These are actual pearls falling from the dhoti! How is that even possible?" She shook her head in disbelief.

Growing up, Hansu had heard stories of such miracles and so she decided to accept the blessing with thankfulness. She collected all the pearls and took them home and put them safely in a big wooden box.

And now the miracle occurred every single day!

Every morning she washed the dhoti and collected the pearls that fell from it. Soon, the

box was full and Hansu decided to sell them in the market. "I am sure these gorgeous pearls will fetch a handsome price from the jeweller. I must check if Saurju needs something."

That afternoon, Hansu went to the market and indeed got a great price for the pristine pearls.

Next morning, at Jaidutt's house, Hansu casually asked him if he needed anything. He was constantly surprised by his younger daughter-in-law's kind and perceptive nature.

By now, Jaidutt felt comfortable sharing his thoughts with Hansu. "Buari, I have been thinking about this one wish that has been playing on my mind for some time. I want to organise a special puja and invite our entire family as well as all the villagers, who are like my extended family. But I guess we will have to wait till my sons come back home. This will require some money and maybe they both can help me out."

Yet again, Hansu managed to surprise her father-in-law as she instantly replied, "Don't worry at all about anything, Saurju. Just leave it to me. I will make all the arrangements and also send out the invitations to everyone."

Hansu got busy with the puja preparations. She cleaned and decorated Jaidutt's home with flowers and drapes. She organised for the priest to conduct the puja and collected all the material needed for the puja. She also invited everyone in their family and village and ordered a delicious feast full of traditional foods and sweets.

All the guests admired the thoughtful arrangements and complimented Jaidutt, "How did you do all this alone and at your age, Jaida?"

"Alone? Not at all. This is all thanks to my Buari, Hansu. She has made all the arrangements to perfection. God bless her!" Jaidutt beamed with pride.

While most of the guests had a great time and thanked Jaidutt and Hansu for their warmth, there was one person who was not feeling all that happy. It was none other than Jaidutt's elder daughter-in-law, Paruli.

Paruli was shocked at the grand event and wondered, "Hmm... No way Hansu could afford all this! Expensive flowers and these fine drapes... and such a large spread of delicacies... All this is way beyond her means... I must find out how she managed to arrange the money for this!"

When Paruli was leaving, she praised the arrangements and invited Hansu for tea to her house the next evening. In all the years they had known each other, Paruli had never been this warm and welcoming. Hansu gladly accepted the invitation and Paruli's change of heart.

When Hansu reached Paruli's home, the latter offered her some hot tea and spicy potato snacks. Paruli was on her best behaviour and she was even smiling for once!

"Here, let me pour you another cup of hot tea, dear sister. Yesterday's event is the talk of the village. But you know me, I worry about you. I worry that Saurju made you spend far more than you could afford for the puja. I hope you were not too careless with your money!"

Hansu smiled and replied, "No, no. Not at all! It was all his money."

But that only baffled Paruli. "Huh! His money? Where did he get this much money?"

Hansu had a pure heart and so she told Paruli the story of the pearls from the dhoti, "... and then I sold the pearls for the puja..."

A new greedy plan was forming in Paruli's mind while she absent-mindedly replied, "That was really very kind of you."

As soon as Hansu finished her story, Paruli placed a hand on her shoulder and said, "You know, I was thinking, since I am the older Buari, actually it is my duty to look after Saurju and take care of him. Don't you worry about him now. From tomorrow, I will go and help him with his chores. You have already done so much for him."

"He is an old man after all. I was just doing whatever I could to make his life easy," said Hansu.

Early next morning, Jaidutt was taken aback to see Paruli instead of Hansu and asked, "Oh! It's you, Paruli. What about Hansu? Why hasn't she come today?"

"Good morning, Saurju! Here, I brought you the Sarayu water for your bath," Paruli said as she put down a small bucket of water. "Hansu wanted to rest. But don't worry, I am here to help you. I will look after you from now on."

She waited impatiently while Jaidutt bathed. She could hear him chant his morning mantras and couldn't help but grumble to herself, "Such long mantras... this is going to take forever... humph... All I want to do is rinse his magical dhoti at the naula and get those pearls Hansu mentioned."

As soon as her father-in-law stepped out of his bath, she almost snatched his used clothes from his hands, including his dhoti.

"I will send back the washed clothes with one of my farm hands."

"But Hansu also prepared my breakf– "

Before Jaidutt could finish what he was saying, Paruli raced down to the naula.

At the naula, she started scrubbing the dhoti while muttering, "Come on! Come on! Show me those precious pearls!"

SCRUB!
SCRUB!
SCRUB!

But, after an hour of vigorous scrubbing and rinsing, the dhoti was in tatters!

As Paruli looked through the gaping hole in the torn dhoti, she decided to give up. She neither sent back the clothes, nor visited Jaidutt again.

After a month, Hansu visited Jaidutt's house and said, "Saurju, how are you? I came to meet you, even though I know that Paruli Didi must be looking after you very well."

But Jaidutt looked bewildered as he said, "Paruli? What are you talking about? I haven't seen her for a month. She hasn't even returned my dhoti."

Hansu was surprised. She immediately offered to help. "Oh, I see! In that case, I will come every morning just like before. Would you like some hot tea?"

"That would be lovely, my dear child!"

Once again, Hansu came every day with a pail of Sarayu water for Jaidutt. And you can be sure that she collected lots and lots of pearls too!

The Lucky Jars

A Folktale from Kerala

FLASH! CRASH! BOOM!

That was the second lightning bolt which had hit dangerously close to the ship's masthead. A loud rumbling echoed through the upper deck of the large wooden merchant ship. Shangren and his crew had set out from the port town of Ningbo in China to India.

Shangren was a successful merchant from China and he had been on several such voyages on the South China Sea and the Pacific Ocean. He would also cross the Indian Ocean to trade with some of the bustling port cities of India.

While he had experienced rough seas before, this time the storm was unrelenting. It had been raining heavily for over a week and the continuous downpour had not only flooded some parts of the ship, but also dampened the spirits of Shangren's crew. They worked day and night to drain out the rainwater as the terrible storm raged on!

This evening, the strong winds were accompanied by massive waves which came crashing down on the ship's front deck. Even Shangren, usually calm in the face of a crisis, looked rattled.

The storm was getting nastier and the ship was swaying worse than ever. Shangren instructed the captain, "Shut the cabin door and move all the expensive cargo to the basement along with all the sailors! Hurry!"

But, in spite of their best efforts, the ship was sinking fast.

"Abandon ship! Abandon ship! We are sinking!" commanded the captain.

Shangren and a few sailors managed to grab some life jackets and jump overboard. Others who were not so lucky slipped and fell into the sea. Shangren was fortunate enough to swim to a smaller rowboat and get inside. He saw

the ship go down along with the brave captain, who continued to help his crew find safety gear until the very last moment.

Shangren struggled to stay afloat in the little boat and started rowing with the single oar he had been able to salvage. He tried to look for other survivors, but unfortunately found none. He somehow managed to reach the shore safely, heartbroken.

Exhausted, he dragged himself out of the boat and onto the sand. He simply lay still for a while, grieving the loss of his crew and cargo.

After some time, he sat up and said a small prayer for the souls of his brave captain and sailors. By now, the storm had passed and it was raining lightly. He looked around and realised that he had reached a coastal village in Kerala. He knew their last location roughly and where they had been shipwrecked and so made an educated guess.

Shangren noticed something else that had also floated ashore – a broken part of the ship. He was pleasantly surprised to find that it contained some of his most precious cargo – ten ornate ceramic jars!

He now felt a glimmer of hope and spotted a humble settlement in the distance. He tied the ten jars with rope, lugged them on his shoulders and decided to ask for help. "I do hope someone lives in that old hut and is able to give me some food and shelter tonight."

The hut belonged to a very poor family. Pandaparrathu Bhattathiri and his wife, Padmini, lived there with their infant daughter.

Most days, they were unable to make ends meet and today was no exception. The husband and wife had just finished feeding the little one and put her to sleep. Bhattathiri was sitting down for dinner, when Padmini came up to him sadly, holding an empty container. "Look! I have used the last bit of rice to make gruel tonight. We will have to figure out something urgently for tomorrow's meal. Sigh!"

Bhattathiri consoled her saying, "Don't despair, my dear. We will figure something out. Tomorrow I will go meet my brother and..." He was interrupted by a loud knock on the door.

Shangren was standing outside, gasping for breath and clutching the ten jars. "Excuse me! Is anybody home? Please open up... I need your help... help me!"

"Oh! I wonder who that poor soul is..." Bhattathiri quickly got up and opened the door.

"My name is Shangren and I am a merchant from China. My ship sank and I lost everything in the storm. I am very tired and hungry as I haven't had anything to eat or drink since yesterday. Please help me..." pleaded the merchant.

Shangren was very weak after his ordeal. Bhattathiri helped him into the house and asked him to sit. Both Bhattathiri and Padmini

were kind-hearted souls and felt sorry for the poor shipwrecked merchant.

They served him the last pot of hot rice gruel, in spite of the fact that they would go hungry that night. "This is all the food we have at home. Please have it."

Shangren ate the gruel hungrily and thanked the two strangers who had showed him such compassion. "You have saved my life! I do not have anything to reward you with right now. But I promise to make up for it on my next visit."

Shangren then extended both his hands to hold Bhattathiri's and continued, "But for now, I need another favour from you. Somehow, miraculously, these ten jars survived the storm and they are very precious to me. I would like

to leave them with you for safekeeping."

"Oh! No, no! My house is too small and old. It is in desperate need of repairs. We cannot keep anything valuable here. I cannot risk its safety," replied Bhattathiri sincerely.

But Shangren insisted, "You misunderstand, my dear man! While the jars are precious to me, they hold nothing very valuable. They are only filled with lentils from my country."

"Well... all right. Since it's just lentils, we will keep them here for you."

Early the next morning, the merchant bid farewell to Bhattathiri and his family and set off on a new journey. Padmini found a suitable spot for the ten ceramic jars in their kitchen and covered them with a sheet of cloth.

Bhattathiri also left home early to seek help

from his brother, who lived in the neighbouring village. The money his brother gave them helped put food on the table for a few weeks, but it ran out soon.

One night, their little daughter was crying and refusing to sleep. Padmini figured that the poor child was just hungry and wanted more food. But whatever little food they had cooked for dinner was over. And there wasn't a single grain of rice left in the house.

Overcome with sadness, Padmini wailed, "This is so unfair. Our little one is hungry and there is nothing to eat in the house. I cannot bear to see her crying face!"

"Let me go see if I can borrow something from Lata Ma," Bhattathiri said and got ready to go to their kindly old neighbour.

"But it's too late to disturb her. She must be sleeping..."

Suddenly Padmini had a thought. "I know what we can do. We can take out a bowl of lentils from the Chinese merchant's jars. I can quickly cook them and feed them to her."

But Bhattathiri was a man of strict principles. He refused, "No, no! How can we do that? Shangren left his jars with us for safekeeping. We cannot use what's inside the jars. It would be wrong!"

Padmini was at her wit's end. "This is not the time to honour your principles! Tell me, is it really a sin, if we take a handful of lentils to feed our starving child? And besides, by the time the merchant returns, we will make sure to replace what we have taken..."

Just then their daughter started bawling even more loudly.

Looking at her tear-streaked face, her father finally caved in. "I guess you are right,

Padmini. As long as we replace the lentils, there is no harm in borrowing."

Bhattathiri went into the kitchen and brought out one jar. He opened it and Padmini used a ladle to scoop some lentils out. However, when she reached into it for a second scoop, the lentils made a curious sound.

CLINK! CLINK!

"I think there is something else in this jar. Let's take a closer look," Padmini suggested as they both peered into the jar.

Padmini held a lamp close to the mouth of the jar. The surface glittered and her jaw dropped!

"Oh dear! There is only a thin layer of lentils on the top of the jar. The rest is filled with gold coins!"

Bhattathiri too was stunned and he immediately checked the remaining nine jars. And sure enough, they too were full of gold coins.

Nervous and astonished, he absent-mindedly started resealing the jars, when Padmini had an idea.

"Listen! Why don't we use just one gold coin for ourselves? We both haven't eaten a full meal in ages!"

"But... but... that... if... if...," tried Bhattathiri, struggling to find the right words.

"Stop 'iffing' and 'butting'! Just take one gold coin and buy some rice, lentils and vegetables from the market. Tonight, we will eat a proper meal... rice, sambar and payasam!"

That night, Bhattathiri and his family ate to

their heart's content and slept peacefully dreaming of delicious food.

Over the next few days, they used the money they got from selling the single gold coin to buy different ingredients and food items and Padmini prepared a variety of traditional delicacies. It was the best week of their lives. With all the feasting, the money soon ran out. Now they would have to go back to living on rice gruel.

Padmini had always been an enterprising young woman and constantly came up with creative ways of making the most of their meagre situation. This time she had a new thought, "What if we take some more gold coins from the jars and sell them? We can use that money to build a better house, start a business, earn money and live comfortably. We can then replace the gold coins with our earnings."

This time, Bhattathiri agreed without a second thought as he felt it was a good idea.

Padmini and Bhattathiri followed their plan to perfection. They built a fine house, started a coconut farming business and made a lot of profit. They also educated their daughter in a good school and helped other less fortunate families.

Eight years later, Bhattathiri and Padmini had not only replaced all the gold coins they had borrowed from the jars, but also filled up ten more small jars with gold coins as interest.

"Life has been good to us. We must always count our blessings!" said Bhattathiri, as he and his wife sat in their front yard admiring their farms.

"You are a good man, my dear. I am grateful for our good fortune," agreed Padmini.

It was a full twelve years before the Chinese merchant, Shangren, returned to their village. This time he was not alone. He came with his crew in tow and another shipload of cargo.

He came to where Bhattathiri's hut had once stood and was surprised to see the spacious mansion in its place.

"Hmm... So, I guess Bhattathiri and his family now live in this huge mansion. He must have found the gold coins in my jars!"

When he went inside and met Bhattathiri and Padmini, he was greeted with the same warmth

with which they had welcomed him long ago on a cold stormy night.

Bhattathiri was delighted to see Shangren and told him all about using some of the gold coins from his jars to start a new life.

"...But, rest assured, I have replaced all the gold coins and have filled ten more small jars as

interest for the coins I took. I hope you are not upset."

"Upset? Not at all. I am very impressed with what

you have managed to do using the gold coins. I do not want the small jars. In fact, I should be paying you for keeping my gold safe for all these years. You are certainly the most honest man I have ever met!"

"But I have made my fortune by investing your gold," Bhattathiri said. "While that may be the case, I did not lose anything by leaving my gold with you. Whatever you have gained from it is because of sheer hard work, good luck and sharp business sense," Shangren replied.

Bhattathiri and Padmini invited the Chinese merchant to stay for lunch and he happily agreed.

Soon it was time to leave. Shangren's crew loaded their cart with the ten ceramic jars from Bhattathiri's home.

The merchant then gifted him one ceramic jar full of gold coins. "This is the reward for your kindness that night, as promised. The mouth of this jar is slightly crooked, but it is a very lucky jar. The house that it is kept in will never want for anything. It will bring you and your family good fortune and abundance for generations to come!"

So it was that once they had used all the gold coins, Bhattathiri began to pickle mangoes and stored them in the lucky Chinese jar. The mango pickle remained forever fresh in the jar and was a sure-fire remedy for loss of appetite.

The pickle became famous and Bhattathiri bought many more jars and made lots of pickle. His new pickle business flourished. Shangren's words had come true.

The lucky Chinese jar became an heirloom and remained in their family for generations as they continued to prosper!

THE GHOST CATCHER

A Folktale from Bengal

Babu the barber and his wife Meena lived in the village of Taklupur. But they were not very happy. While Babu was a very skilled barber, there was never enough work in his village. Taklupur was a unique place. It had a good number of bald people. Very few people needed haircuts and so the barber did not make much money. In fact, Babu and Meena barely had enough to eat on most days.

The barber's wife would complain to him every single day. "If you didn't have the means to support a family, why did you marry me?" she would ask crossly.

"At my parents' house, I had large scrumptious spreads almost every day... Oh, how I miss... aloo dum... maach bhaat... and mishti... my favourite..." she yearned.

One warm afternoon, when the barber was blissfully napping in the courtyard, Meena lost her patience. In a fit of anger, she ran after her husband with a broomstick. She chased him all around the house, yelling, "You lazy fellow! Are you ever going to find a job that pays?"

"Meenaaa...listennn... I have some clever ideas... I was..." tried Babu.

But Meena interrupted him, "Clever ideas? What should I do with your clever ideas? Eat them with rice?" she cried, still chasing him.

After this broomstick incident, the barber felt very insulted. He packed up his tools and decided to set out in search of work.

"I will only see your face when I become rich!" promised a humiliated Babu before leaving.

"Humph!" scoffed Meena.

As the barber did not have much hope of finding work in his own village, he decided to try his luck in the next one. When he entered Keshpur, he was delighted to see the village people.

The people of Keshpur had lots and lots of hair...

Straight hair, curly hair, short hair, long hair, thin hair, thick hair...

It was a barber's dream come true.

Babu was convinced that he was about to make a fortune in Keshpur. He stopped and offered his services to a man sporting a very long unkempt beard.

The man laughed out loud and said, "My dear fellow, in Keshpur we believe that hair is a divine gift. Surely, we won't go around cutting our divine gifts, would we now?"

And so, a disappointed Babu decided to go to the next village instead.

Swayampur was only an hour away. It was a quaint little village with brightly coloured houses.

Babu spotted a wise-looking lady tending to her garden. "Namaste. My name is Babu and I am very talented."

"Yes, yes... we all are," she replied absent-mindedly.

"Um... no, I meant... I am a skilled barber and I am here to offer my hair-cutting services," added Babu hopefully.

"Ah... but in Swayampur we all are skilled barbers. In fact, we are skilled at everything... we are all barbers, gardeners, builders, tailors, swimmers..." explained the lady. "Out here, it is our custom to do all our work ourselves. See, I have grown these flowers all on my own!" she said proudly.

"Right!" remarked Babu and turned around to leave Swayampur. He went to a few more villages but had no luck whatsoever. At nightfall, Babu reached the outskirts of a forest. He was tired, hungry and dispirited.

He lay down to rest under a tamarind tree. Soon, he fell asleep and started to mumble, "Trim... hair... bald... money... beard..."

These words caught the attention of a young ghost who lived on this tree. He peered at Babu from the branches and smacked his lips.

"Just what I need. A midnight snack!" thought the young ghost.

The ghost climbed down and came close to the sleeping man. He looked at his chunky ankles. "He will do nicely... very nicely indeed!" said the young ghost with glee.

So, the young ghost made a dramatic entry in his ghostly style. With outspread arms and a gaping mouth, he jumped in front of the sleeping barber and bellowed. "YOUR TIME IS UP! I AM GOING TO EAT YOU! NOBODY CAN SAVE YOU NOW!"

MWAH HA HA HA HA!

Babu woke up with a fright...

GASP!

... and jumped out of his skin.

He saw a truly horrifying sight in front of him – a pale, towering ghost with lanky limbs and long slender fingers. As the young ghost took a step closer, Babu started shaking from head to toe and his hair stood on end.

"Now, now... where should I start... chubby arms... bony fingers... or crunchy toes?" the young ghost wondered loudly.

The young ghost looked even scarier up close. He had yellow eyes with a deathly stare and his teeth looked sharp and pointy.

"I... I... please... don't..." tried Babu, but no words came out.

A chill ran down his spine, but the barber

had to think fast if he wanted to survive this terrible fate.

At first his mind went blank, but then Babu had an idea!

He mustered up all his courage and said in a steady voice, "O silly spirit, try if you must! But you won't succeed, as I am no ordinary barber. Do you know what's in my bag?"

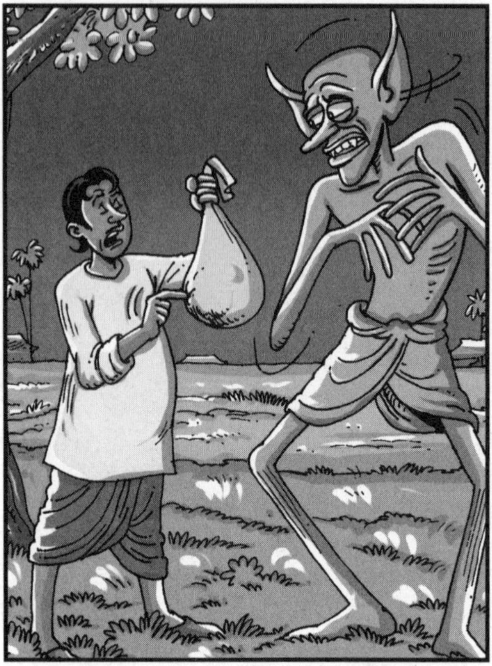

The ghost looked confused as Babu continued, "I have trapped many a ghost inside this. And they were bigger, scarier and toothier than you."

The ghost looked bewildered.

HUH!

"But that is a very small bag to fit so many ghosts as you claim," the young ghost asked suspiciously.

Babu pulled out a rectangular mirror from his bag of tools and held it in front of the young ghost's face.

"Look! This is the face of the last ghost I captured tonight before meeting you. Counting you, I will have trapped fifty ghosts just this week," said the barber with an evil grin.

But the young ghost still looked doubtful and Babu knew he had to act quickly.

So, the barber pulled out a comb and said, "And in case you were wondering, this is what I use to straighten out the ghosts."

And then he took out his largest pair of scissors and added, "And with this I trim the ghosts so that they fit neatly inside my ghost catcher!"

The barber made an ominous snipping sound with his scissors.

SNIP! SNIP!

"Now, now... where should I start... lanky legs... uneven fingers... or pointy ears?" the barber wondered loudly.

The young ghost was convinced and believed every word the barber had spoken.

Now, he was scared and willing to do anything to avoid being straightened, trimmed and bagged!

"Oh, Sir Barber... I am but a young ghost just learning how to haunt... I will give you whatever you want! Please... please don't trap me," he begged.

"No. I would rather meet my ghost quota for the week," replied Babu firmly.

The young ghost was now even more terrified. He had to somehow plead his case.

"Sir Barber... I am a ghost of many talents and I haunt just the right places, including the Queen's palace! I can be very useful to you."

"But you ghosts are a deceitful lot. Why should I trust you?"

"I... I am willing to do anything... any task... whatever you need done... right away..." stuttered the young ghost.

"Oh, all right! I can make an exception for you, I suppose. Let's see if you are as good as your word. First, go and get me one thousand gold mohurs right away. But remember, if you fail, I will bag you!" warned the barber.

"As you wish, Sir Barber!" said the young ghost and left immediately.

He promptly reached the Queen's palace and terrorised the guards at the palace treasury.

Mission accomplished, the young ghost returned to the tamarind tree with a bag filled with a thousand gold mohurs.

As he handed it to Babu, the barber's eyes gleamed and he knew that finally his luck had turned.

Feeling confident that the young ghost had believed his bluff, Babu gave him a second task. "Now that you have passed the test, go build a granary at my house in Taklupur. Make sure that it's ready by tomorrow night and filled with paddy. Am I clear?"

"Yes, Sir Barber. As you wish," said the young ghost meekly.

The next morning, the barber joyfully returned home with a jingling bag of gold mohurs.

Meena, who had been worried about her husband, breathed a sigh of relief when she saw Babu.

She ran to greet him and apologised for her outburst. Babu smiled and showed her the bag of gold mohurs.

"O Ma! Is that really... gold...?" she gasped in disbelief.

Babu told her about his encounter with the young ghost and how he had not only escaped a painful death but also made a fortune out of the tricky situation.

Meena was happy to see him back home and delighted that now they were rich.

The same night, the young ghost turned up at the barber's house to build him a granary as commanded.

The poor young ghost was so scared of being put into the bag that he worked without a single break and finished building the granary in record time.

He was carrying large sheaves of paddy, when his uncle, an old ghost, came by.

"Why exactly are you carrying such heavy sheaves of paddy on your back?" asked the confused old ghost.

"Shush! Uncle, please speak softly or he will hear us!" whispered the young ghost, who was dripping with sweat and fear.

"He? Who's he?" asked the old ghost.

The young ghost told his uncle about his terrible misfortune – how a seemingly harmless midnight snack had turned into a never-ending nightmare.

The old ghost was aghast. "You gullible fool! You really think the barber can bag you?"

"Uncle, don't doubt the power of this barber. He is a very skilled ghost catcher. He even showed me the face of the last ghost he had bagged," replied the young ghost with a shudder.

"What nonsense! Bah!" dismissed the old ghost.

"You don't believe me? Come and see for yourself," offered the young ghost.

The ghosts headed straight to the barber's bedroom window. They brought with them a strong cold gust of wind which slammed the window open.

Babu sat up in his bed. "Oh... what was that!"

When he looked out of the window, he saw not one but two ghosts approaching him swiftly. He acted quickly and dug out the mirror from his tool bag. He flashed the mirror in their direction and both the ghosts were startled to see their own reflections.

"Aha! It's my lucky night. Two ghosts together! Come now, let's make this quick. Let's bag both of you so that I can go back to sleep," said Babu loudly in a threatening voice.

Both the young and the old ghost were petrified.

EEEEEP!

GULP!

"Please don't trap me! I am an old and weary ghost. Have some mercy!" pleaded the old ghost.

The barber continued to hold the mirror in front of the ghosts. "No mercy for you! You disturbed my sleep and now you must pay!"

Both the ghosts shuddered.

But the old ghost quickly offered, "I... I will build another granary for you and fill it up with wheat."

"Oh, all right! I can make another exception, I suppose. Now get to work!" ordered Babu.

The two ghosts built a second granary that night and were never to be seen again.

In just two nights, the barber and his wife had not only acquired one thousand gold mohurs, but they also had two large granaries filled with paddy and wheat.

The barber became a rich trader in grain and Meena no longer complained.

They both lived happily ever after in Taklupur.

And from that day on, Babu the trader never left home without his trusty 'Ghost Catcher' tools just in case he met another ghost or someone needed a haircut.

The Man, The Tiger and The Jackal

A Folktale from Punjab

Jagat was a man of many qualities. He was caring, helpful and very hardworking. But brave, he was not!

There is a famous saying, "Bravery is not the absence of fear, but the mastery of it." And it would be accurate to say that Jagat was not only easily afraid but also a slave to his fear.

Jagat was a priest by profession. He spent most of his time carrying out ceremonies at the behest of the village people. His fear did not leave much room for adventure and Jagat was more than happy leading his humdrum life.

One day, he received an important letter in the mail. It was an invitation from his youngest sister for the naming ceremony of her newborn daughter. It was going to be a grand celebration and Jagat's sister had insisted on his presence on the auspicious day.

But there was one problem. His sister lived in the village across the mountains, which was accessible through only one route. The road passed through a dense forest and so far, Jagat had managed to avoid a journey through it.

Though Jagat loved his sister and really wanted to go, he was hesitant. His wife calmed his nerves and encouraged him to go. And so, it was decided that Jagat would leave early the next morning.

At the break of dawn, the priest started his long journey on foot along the path that went through the forest around the mountain. He was carrying only a small bag. A change of clothes, some snacks and a gift for his little niece was all he really needed for the occasion.

For most of the morning, his walk was pleasant and filled with some mesmerising sights and scenes of the forest. Evergreen trees, gushing waterfalls and cool breeze kept him company. The sound of chirping birds and the scent of fragrant flowers soothed his senses and Jagat felt all his fears disappear.

But not for long. Shortly after, he turned a corner on the grassy path and heard some grunting sounds coming from behind a tree. He walked towards it and saw a truly terrifying sight!

A muscular, brightly striped tiger was trapped inside a bamboo cage.

EEEEP!

Jagat let out a high-pitched cry. The tiger turned and looked at Jagat's frightened face.

But instead of a looking fierce, the tiger seemed scared and sad.

"Help! Please, please help me! Let me out. I beg you, my dear man!" pleaded the tiger.

But "Err... Umm..." is all Jagat could muster up.

"Please have some mercy. I have been trapped here since last night and not a soul has walked by who could have helped me. Now that you are finally here, please set me free!" urged the tiger.

Finally, Jagat managed to gather his senses and his kind-heartedness got the better of him.

"Of course, of course. I would really like to help you..." his voice trailed off.

"Then what are you waiting for, my dear man? Just unlock this door, right here!" the tiger said, gesturing towards the cage door.

Jagat cleared his throat and spoke up, "But if I let you out, you will definitely eat me!"

"I give you my honest word, that will never happen. I will be indebted to you forever," promised the tiger.

Jagat had half a mind to walk away, but he was a priest and an earnest one at that! He took his duty to help all living creatures very seriously.

And so, he decided to put the poor tiger out of his misery.

"Please remember your promise," Jagat requested as he opened the cage door.

But a tiger doesn't change his stripes for anyone!

As soon as he stepped out of the bamboo cage, the tiger took a threatening step towards Jagat and bared his teeth. "Ha! You really are a very foolish and gullible man, aren't you! But you will certainly make for a delicious meal!"

Jagat was shocked and froze with fear. A few seconds passed and he managed to take a deep breath. "Please, you gave me your word! You said you would be thankful for my help..."

"Oh that! I would have promised anything to be set free. You can't possibly take what I said so seriously!" replied the tiger as he took another ominous step towards Jagat.

Jagat took two steps back and was now pressed up against a tree trunk.

"And I am very thankful, but I am also very hungry!" added the tiger, coming closer.

"Please, Sir, find some kindness in your heart. I have a loving family I need to get back to. Please spare me!" begged the priest, down on his knees.

"Don't grovel. I prefer my food standing up

straight!" the tiger roared.

But seeing the poor priest trembling, the tiger finally said, "Oh, all right! I will give you one chance. Go ahead and ask the first three things you meet whether I should let you go. Even if one of them agrees, I will let you live."

Jagat somehow stood up straight and looked towards his right. He saw an enormous, old, wise-looking tree nearby and decided to ask her. It was mid-day and the sun was shining brightly. Jagat was blinded by it, but he ran as fast as his legs could carry him.

"Good afternoon, Madam Tree! I have an important question which needs your guidance and my life literally depends on it!" he greeted the old tree.

"Sure. It's not like I have anywhere to go," replied Madam Tree, looking a bit bored.

Jagat narrated the whole saga of how on his way to his sister's house, he encountered a trapped tiger and set him free as he believed the tiger's promise of sparing his life.

"... And so, what do you think, Madam Tree?

Shouldn't the tiger keep his word and let me live? It only seems fair..." asked Jagat hopefully.

"Well... it's not that simple. The

world isn't a fair place. I think the tiger should eat you!" Madam Tree said dismissively.

"But, Madam Tree, doesn't gratitude mean anything?"

"One would think it means something, wouldn't one! But look at me for instance. I generously give weary travellers my shade to rest and share my fruit with them. And what do they do in return? They just keep cutting down my branches without even a second thought. So, why shouldn't the tiger eat you?"

Disappointed by Madam Tree's answer, Jagat turned to his left this time.

In the distance, he saw a field where an ox was tied to a water wheel and decided to try his luck there instead.

The poor ox looked exhausted as he had been working hard all morning without a single break.

He was slowly trudging along when Jagat approached him.

"Hello, my good Sir! I need your help on a matter of life and death!"

"Humph! A man needs help. Tell me something new!" grunted the ox, rolling his eyes sarcastically.

Jagat explained his predicament and asked the ox for his kind opinion.

"My kindest opinion is that you are a massive fool! Your stupidity knows no bounds if

you expect compassion from anyone, let alone a tiger!" yelled the disgruntled ox.

"Oh... but I trusted the

tiger's promise..." said the priest, only to be interrupted by the wrath of the old ox.

"Bah! Promises are the sweetest lies, I tell you. I have heard them all my life. When I was young and could plough the fields, the farmer fed me the finest cotton seeds and loads of delightful oil cakes. He even promised to look after me and keep me well-fed. But now that I am old, I am tied to a yoke and given only dry fodder!"

"So yes, the tiger should eat you! This world is unfair and promises are meant to be broken!" the ox ranted on.

"Oh!" thought Jagat, as his chances of staying alive became bleaker.

He walked away from the field towards the nearest path. With one last burst of hope, he decided to ask the road on which he was walking. He shared his sob story with the road and asked for his view.

"Alas, you are doomed! The tiger is definitely going to eat you!"

"But... why? Shouldn't the tiger let me live in exchange for the kindness I have shown him?"

"Look at me! All day long, everybody — rich and poor, young and old — walks and tramples all over me. Nobody ever spares me a thought. I am so useful and what do I get in exchange? Some stomps and plods?" complained
the road.

Dismayed by this response, the priest gave up. "Maybe everyone is right, after all. Let the tiger just eat me."

Jagat turned back sadly and with his head down started walking towards where the tiger was waiting. Suddenly, he heard a cheerful voice. He looked up to see a jackal.

"Why so sad, my dear man? What seems to be the matter?"

The priest repeated his story one more time and declared how his fate was sealed. But the jackal seemed very confused.

"Wait. So, there's a man, a tiger, a cage and a bamboo?"

"No. Just a man, a tiger and a bamboo cage. Not a separate bamboo," Jagat clarified.

"How very confusing! Would you please tell me once again?"

After Jagat had explained the whole situation once again, the jackal looked even more puzzled.

"Everything seems so mixed up. So, you are telling me that a tiger put you in a cage?"

"No, no. Why would I be in a cage?" Jagat cried in exasperation.

But the jackal continued, "It's not making any sense to me. Maybe if you take me to the place where all this happened, perhaps I would understand it better."

So, the priest and the jackal reached the spot near the bamboo cage where the tiger was waiting rather impatiently.

"It's way past my lunch time. Where have you been?" grumbled the tiger. "Ah! Never mind, let's just get started."

"Do give me just a few more minutes. I am trying to explain the situation to this slow-witted jackal," Jagat said, gesturing towards the jackal.

The jackal ignored the tiger and continued talking, "So, you were saying you were lying down?"

"No! When did I say that? I said I was walking, and the tiger was in the cage!"

"You were in the cage and you wanted to eat the tiger? I don't understand."

Now, Jagat was really riled up and frantically trying to explain, "No! No! Look! I was walking past the cage and..."

The tiger finally lost his patience and roared, "ENOUGH! STOP THIS NONSENSE!"

"You are such a fool! I will eat you too!" he added, glaring at the jackal.

"Sssssorry... Please don't eat me. I completely understand now. I was in the cage... no... you wanted to eat the cage! Wait, how can that be?" mumbled the jackal. "You were talking... and the cage walked by... Oh dear! I will never be able to understand this!"

ARGGGHHH!!!

The tiger was not one to suffer fools!

"Listen up! I will explain this only once and you will have to understand," he commanded and started telling the story from the beginning.

When he finished, the jackal said, "Oh... I get it now. You were inside this cage?"

The tiger walked into the cage to demonstrate his point. "Yes! I was inside the cage. Look!"

The jackal took this chance, quickly leapt forward and slammed the cage shut.

"And that's where you shall remain!" he said, grinning.

"ROAR! Let me out, you tricksters. NOW!"

While the tiger bellowed, Jagat and the jackal walked away as fast as they could.

The priest thanked the jackal for saving his life and praised his quick-thinking.

The jackal asked smugly, "So, do you still think I am slow-witted?"

"I think you are the cleverest animal in the whole wide world!"

The priest and the jackal walked together until Jagat reached his sister's village. And in this way, the priest's adventure ended on a happy note and it was the first of many more to come!

FAVOURITE INDIAN FOLKTALES

WRITTEN BY

NALINI SORENSEN

Janba's Buffalo

A Folktale from Maharashtra

Janba Patil was a true family man. He adored his wife, Janai, and his two children, Rahul and Reena. He was a devoted husband and a very loving father. The family lived in a small village in Maharashtra. They led a simple, honest life. They didn't have a lot of money, but they made do with what they had and life was fairly good for them.

Everyone in the village knew that Janba was a helpful, hardworking man, with a kind heart. Because of his trusting and compassionate nature, it was often quite easy to fool him. But Janba didn't mind. He was always willing to help a person in need and went out of his way to do good deeds for others.

The family had just finished eating a meal of spicy potato curry, rice and pickle one night,

when Janai yawned loudly and sighed. Janba was about to tease her, when he noticed that Janai looked exhausted.

"That was delicious," he said, with a smile, washing his fingers. "You always know just how much spice to add to a curry."

"I know it is your favourite, Janba," replied Janai.

"It is. But what is it, Janai? Why do you look so tired tonight?" asked Janba, barely able to hide his concern.

"It's hard work looking after two buffaloes, the home and also our children, Janba. They are growing up so fast. They need a lot more of my attention," she replied.

"I understand," said Janba. "What if I–"

"I was thinking," interrupted Janai. "What if we sell one of the buffaloes? We need just one. That would reduce my work here at home for sure."

"That actually is a good idea! Better than the one I had, anyway. We'll keep Gollu and sell Bollu. Let me take him to the market tomorrow morning and sell him. He is strong and healthy. He would be a blessing on any farm. We should be able to get a good price for him," replied Janba, happily.

Janba woke up early the next morning. He quickly drank his tea and ate a few rotis. Then,

before it got too hot, he waved goodbye to Janai, Rahul and Reena, and set off towards the market, with Bollu, the buffalo.

He had barely walked fifteen minutes, when he bumped into Kawade, an old acquaintance from the village.

"Hello Janba! Where are you going so bright and early this morning?" asked Kawade, with a smile on his face.

"Hello Kawade," replied Janba. "Good morning! I'm taking Bollu, our buffalo, to the market to sell him. Janai is finding it hard to manage the children, the home and two buffaloes."

"Is that so? Why go all the way to the market? I can exchange my fine horse for your buffalo right here, Janba. I can save you the trip."

Janba was delighted. "That would be great! Thank you so much. I know my children would be thrilled with a horse. They would love to learn to ride it," he replied, already hearing the cheers of glee from his children.

The deal was done, the men shook hands and Kawade went briskly on his way.

Janba sat astride the horse, and they started to go on their way. But in just a few seconds he realised why Kawade had been keen to exchange him.

"This horse is lame! Kawade!" he yelled.

But Kawade was out of sight. And even if he could hear Janba's shouts, he wasn't about to appear.

Janba got off the horse. He lovingly patted its head. The horse nuzzled his hand. It could feel Janba's kindness.

"Don't worry. I will take you to the market and we will see if we can have someone look at your hoof," whispered Janba.

Janba and the horse started walking slowly towards the market. As they reached the outskirts of the village, they met the grocery shop owner, Nene.

"Good morning, Janba," he greeted him warmly. "Are you on your way to the market to sell that poor, lame horse?"

"Maybe, Nene," Janba sighed. "I was thinking of taking it to get its leg attended to first..."

"It'll take you the entire day to reach the market, Janba. If you like, I can exchange your lame horse for my frisky goat. I was also on my way to the market to sell it," replied Nene.

"Oh, thank you!" said Janba. "I know that Janai would find it much easier to take care of a goat than a horse."

The deal was done, the men shook hands and Nene was on his way.

However, Janba had barely walked five minutes, before the goat collapsed to the ground, with a small thud.

"Oh no!" exclaimed Janba. "This goat isn't well!"

Janba lovingly patted the goat on its head, right between its horns, and whispered, "Don't worry, dear goat. I'll take you to a vet. Hang in there, little one."

The goat rubbed its head on Janba's leg. It could feel Janba's kindness.

Janba bent down and carried the goat in his arms. And he started on the long walk to the market. As he neared the market, he could feel the muscles in his arms hurting. He was just contemplating taking a small rest, when he bumped into two villagers.

"Janba! It's been a long while. How are you?" one greeted him.

"What's happened to your goat?" asked the other.

"The goat isn't feeling well. I was planning on taking it to the vet, and then selling it," replied Janba.

"Oh, I have an idea," said the first villager. "Why don't we exchange my rooster for your goat? You can easily sell the rooster and it will save you time at the vet. We just walked past there and there's a long wait at the clinic. It'll take you a couple of hours at least. There's a long line of animals waiting to be attended to."

The deal was done and before they could even shake hands, the two villagers disappeared. Janba looked down at the plump rooster in his arms. He looked back at him through beady

eyes, ruffling his feathers. His comb glistened under the rays of the sun.

"Oh god," he said to the rooster. "What a day it's been! My big Bollu has turned into you! A rooster! And I have no money and nothing to eat. Nothing to show for this."

The rooster cocked his head to one side and clucked loudly.

"No, no! Not your fault, I know," whispered Janba to him. "But I need to sell you, my friend. I don't have a choice."

The rooster leant his head on Janba's chest. He could feel Janba's kindness. Janba patted his head and, dragging his feet, slowly walked to the poultry shop.

"All I can give you for this rooster is fifty rupees," said the poultry shop owner, in a rude, bossy tone. "Take it or leave it."

Janba was hungry and tired. He knew that he was in no position to bargain with him. He took the money and handed over the rooster with a final loving pat on his head. Then Janba crossed the street and went to a tiny shop selling parcels of rice, dal and vegetables. He was starving after the long walk, and his arms ached after carrying the heavy goat.

He sat on the grass, leant his back against a peepal tree and sighed. He was just opening the package of food, when a poor, hungry man walked up to him.

"Please, sir. Please give me your food. I have not eaten in days. My stomach hurts. I don't know for how much longer I can carry on," said the man.

Janba's heart melted. He didn't even wait to think it through.

"Sure. I don't have much. But you look like you need it more than I do. You can have it," replied Janba, handing over the parcel of food.

"Oh, thank you, sir. You are so kind. May god bless you immensely," replied the poor, hungry man, his eyes shining.

Janba smiled. He turned around and started on the long walk back home. He reached just as the sun was going down. As he walked through the door, Rahul and Reena screamed with joy and ran into his arms; their daily ritual, whenever Janba returned home. Janai watched the three of them, with love. After things had calmed down and the children had gone to play with their toys, Janai asked him, "Janba, did you get a good price for Bollu?"

"Well, it's been a long day. I exchanged Bollu for a horse," replied Janba.

"A horse? Where is it? That's great news. Rahul and Reena would love to ride a horse," said Janai.

"I exchanged the horse for a goat," said Janba.

"A goat? Well, that's not bad either. A goat is far less work than a buffalo or a horse," said Janai.

"Oh, Janai! There's more. Then I exchanged the goat for a rooster," said Janba.

"That's excellent! A rooster can wake us all up bright and early each morning!" said Janai.

"No wait. Don't get excited. I sold the rooster. I was so tired and hungry. I used some of the money to buy some food," Janba continued.

"That's okay, Janba. Don't worry about it. At least you got a meal and some money," Janai replied, putting an arm around her husband's shoulder.

"No, Janai. You don't understand. As I sat down to eat, a poor, hungry man came by, asking for food. I couldn't bear to eat when he looked like he hadn't eaten in days. So, I gave him the food," said Janba. "I'm sorry."

"Janba, what are you sorry for? You are such a kind person, truly. That was such a good thing to do. There is no greater act of kindness than sharing food. You must be starving. Let me cook something quickly for you," said Janai.

Janba silently thanked the gods for his understanding wife. He ate his dinner with relish, and went off to bed. He was tired after the long, eventful trip to the market.

"Cookadooodledooooo!"

Janba jumped out of his bed with a start, the next morning. He opened the front door and there was a surprise waiting for him!

"Janai! Rahul! Reena! Wake up! Come soon!" he yelled, unable to believe his eyes.

The family gathered at the door and looked in wonder at their buffalo, Bollu, the horse, the goat, the rooster and a pile of gold coins right in front of them.

"It's a miracle!" exclaimed Janai. "I think you have been blessed for your kindness yesterday, Janba."

Rahul and Reena screamed with joy and ran towards the four animals.

The Fake Astrologer

A Folktale from Bengal

Goopi and his wife, Koki, lived in a remote village in Bengal. While Koki was a simple, hardworking woman, Goopi was, admittedly, just a little bit lazy. It got on Koki's nerves.

One morning, she woke up even before the sun rose. She made her way to the well, waited in line for her turn and labouriously pulled up two pots full of water. Then she balanced one on her head, the other on her hip, and slowly made her way back home, trying hard not to spill the water. The sun now shone fiercely on her as she walked. She reached home exhausted, only to find Goopi still sleeping on the mat on the floor.

"Wake up, Goopi!" she exclaimed. "It is mid-morning. How can you still be sleeping? You did nothing yesterday. How can you be so tired?"

Goopi lifted his arms over his head, stretched his body and slowly sat up. He rubbed his eyes and yawned. Then he slowly got up from the mattress and walked into the kitchen, where he knew he'd find Koki. Koki was a splendid cook. She tempered the food with just the perfect amount of spices, and Goopi could feel his stomach rumbling.

"Good morning, Koki. I'm a bit hungry. Will you make me idlis for breakfast, please?" he asked, politely.

"Goopi! There is not a single grain of rice in our home.

I scraped the last grains out of the jar for our dinner yesterday. We are out of food. You will need to go to the village or the neighbouring villages and earn us some money so we can buy some more rice and dal. We've finished the vegetables that I grew in the patch outside too. You need to earn some money for me to make you those idlis," replied his wife. The desperation and weariness came through in her voice. Goopi knew she was right.

Goopi freshened up and slunk out of the house. He knew that Koki had every reason to be upset with him. He knew they needed some money to buy provisions. He'd gone too long without working and earning any money.

He reached the village square and found work stringing marigolds into garlands, at a stall outside the temple. He had barely got the hang of it, when the woman who had employed him said, "Goopi, you are poking the flowers too hard! They are wilting even before the garland is ready. This is not the right job for you."

Dejected, Goopi walked on towards the next village. There, he found work carrying stones for the construction of a large house on the outskirts. But that didn't work out either. The stones were heavy, and Goopi could not carry too many at once. The supervisor soon said to him, "Goopi, if you only carry one stone on your head, this house will never be completed! We have a schedule to keep!"

Goopi was very disheartened. He dragged his feet over to the foot of a banyan tree. He sat in its shade and considered his options. He really didn't know what he could do, and he did not want to go back home to Koki with no money in his pockets.

Just then, a sadhu happened to pass by. He couldn't help but notice Goopi sitting under the tree, completely defeated. "You look worried, my friend. What seems to be the matter?" he asked him, compassionately.

Goopi told him his story.

"Come with me, my child. Come to my ashram. I will help you," said the sadhu.

Goopi was very grateful. He walked with the sadhu to the ashram.

Goopi soon got used to life in the ashram. The day followed a fixed timetable. The sadhu woke the young men training to become sadhus and hermits very early each morning, even before sunrise. They first prayed, then they exercised. Right after that they bathed, followed by breakfast. Then they studied the religious scriptures till lunch.

After lunch, there was a short time for some rest, then some prayers and then more studies. It was soon tea time and, after that, the young men all had to pitch in and cook dinner. The tasks were evenly divided among them. Dinner was eaten early, just after sundown, followed by prayers, and they were off to bed. Only to do the same thing all over again the next day. It was a strict, disciplined life, and Goopi resigned himself to it.

Life would have been good, if it weren't for one tiny detail. Goopi didn't know how to read or write. The sadhu soon noticed this and took him under his wing. He tutored him personally. Goopi was intelligent and took it all in like a sponge. Within ten days he had mastered the letters of the alphabet. The sadhu was very proud of him.

"Goopi, you have learnt the letters of the alphabet so fast! You are really intelligent. Tomorrow I will teach you how to string letters together to make words. You seem to be a natural. You will pick it up fast," said the sadhu.

This compliment went straight to Goopi's head. He was thrilled. He'd always fancied himself to be an intellectual and here was proof! He knew the sadhu could impart even more knowledge to him, but Goopi couldn't see himself staying at the ashram for much longer.

For many days now, he had missed his village, and he had missed Koki. He was not used to such a disciplined life. Besides, if he was indeed so intelligent, he could figure out words on his own. He didn't need the sadhu. That night as he lay on his mat on the hard floor, he found it hard to sleep. All these thoughts swirled around in his head, and he tossed and turned.

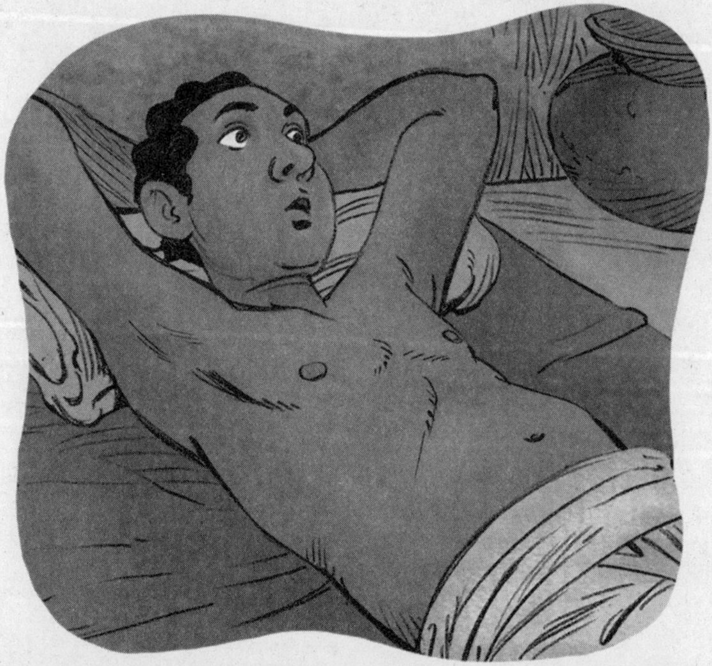

He woke up the next morning and went straight to meet the sadhu. "Guruji, I am grateful for the knowledge you have imparted, but I feel I have a greater calling," said Goopi.

"Eh? Calling? What do you mean?" asked the sadhu, puzzled.

"The time has come for me to leave. Greater things await me, Guruji," he replied.

Nothing the sadhu said could convince Goopi to stay. He was soon on his way.

With a bounce in his step he started walking away from the ashram. *Nobody in my village will understand my greatness and my intelligence. I must go straight to King Deviya. He will appreciate me as the embodiment of knowledge that I truly am,* he thought as he walked.

His intention was to go directly to the palace, but something distracted him. He was passing by his own village when he noticed a delicious aroma wafting through the air. He lifted his nose up in the air and followed the trail... only to realise that it was coming from his own house. It was Koki! Koki was cooking boras (fritters made with sugar palm). Goopi was sure of it. He had a keen sense of smell and his nose never lied.

He went straight inside his house, without so much as knocking. "Koki! Koki! It is me! How are you?" he asked his wife.

"You are back! Welcome home, Goopi. I have missed you. Have you earned any money?" asked Koki.

"I have returned home after gaining immense knowledge from a great sage, Koki. Your husband is the greatest intellectual in this village!" Goopi exclaimed.

"Goopi, don't say all these things. I have borrowed money from our neighbour to make ends meet. We still don't have any provisions at home. What is this intellect you are talking about? I don't believe you!" said Koki, confused.

"You don't believe me? You want to test my powers? Listen to me, here's how I can convince you. I know exactly what you were cooking just before I got here," said Goopi. Then he paused dramatically, closed his eyes and pretended to be channeling some unknown energy. He slowly said, "You were frying boras."

Koki was astounded! She completely believed that her husband now had some new magical powers. "Goopi! Wow! How did you... ?"

"There! There! There! Are you convinced now? You see I've changed? I have a great bank of knowledge within me now. My guruji gave me powers. Now, I am a... a... an astrologer! From today, everyone shall only call me Pandit Goopi," said Goopi, making this up on the spur of the moment. He liked how the words 'astrologer' and 'pandit' rolled off his tongue. "Please now, Koki, go and bring me some boras."

Koki immediately went to fry some boras for him. As he chewed his food, Goopi's head buzzed with thoughts... *I am in fact an astrologer and it is important that I play the part right from day one, now that I am back home. If I could convince Koki so easily, I can convince the rest of the village just as easily.*

As soon as he finished eating, Goopi got a mat and sat cross-legged on it. He smeared some

ash on his forehead. He closed his eyes and sat on the mat in a deep meditative trance, his back erect. He was fully aware that Koki would be looking at him.

Koki called her neighbour over. "Just look at him," she whispered, hiding behind the door.

"I just can't believe my eyes! He used to be so lazy," replied the neighbour.

"He is meditating. He is a pandit! An astrologer!" declared Koki, proudly.

In no time at all, word travelled through the village and to the neighbouring villages as well. There were lines of people waiting outside Koki and Goopi's home, to receive help and guidance from Pandit Goopi.

"When will my daughter get married, Panditji?" asked one.

"Will my business turn around, Panditji?" asked another, hopefully.

"Will my father recover completely from this accident, Panditji?" asked a third.

And our fake astrologer imparted fake advice and predictions, left, right and centre. Soon, as his customers increased, he became a wealthy man. Pandit Goopi and Koki were even able to move into a larger, more comfortable house. Those days of poverty and no provisions

became a distant memory. Life was good. The kitchen was always full of delicious food, bubbling on the stove.

One morning, Pandit Goopi awoke to loud cries. "Panditji! Panditji!"

He got out of bed and went to open the door. "Who are you? Why have you disturbed my... err... umm... prayers? And my meditation?" he asked.

"Please forgive me, Panditji. I am Moti. I am a washerman from the next village. I left my home at sunrise to come here to you. I urgently need your help, Panditji," said Moti.

"What is it? What seems to be the problem?" asked Pandit Goopi.

"Panditji, it's my donkey. He's been missing since last evening. I have looked for him everywhere, but I can't find him. Without him

my business will die! I need the donkey to help me carry the clothes from house to house. I cannot carry the weight myself. Please use your powers and bring him back to me. I will give you all the money I have," said Moti, almost in tears.

"Hmmm..." said Pandit Goopi. "Let me see what I can do. Why don't you wait here, while I go for a little meditative walk?"

Pandit Goopi went on a short walk, all the while hoping that he would see the donkey somewhere along the path. Animals don't usually stray far from their owners, he knew that. But there was no sign of the donkey. The entire time Pandit Goopi was trying to think of what he should say to Moti.

When he returned home, Moti was waiting for him. He joined his hands and asked, "Panditji, did you find my donkey?"

If I tell him that I failed, he will make fun of me and word will get out in the village, thought

Pandit Goopi. He knew he had to lie.

"Moti, the truth of the matter is Goddess Chandi is punishing you for the bad deeds of your past life and has taken your donkey away from you. I will try to appease her during my prayers and meditation today. But this might take some time. Go home now. Come back tomorrow. Leave me to it," said Pandit Goopi.

That very night, when Pandit Goopi and Koki were deep in sleep, Koki woke up to some scratching sounds outside their house.

"Wake up, Goopi," Koki said, shaking him. "What are those sounds? Is it a thief?"

"There is a sound! What can it be?" asked Pandit Goopi, still half asleep. "W-wh-who... who is out there?"

There was no reply, but the scratching sounds seemed to get louder.

"Let me go get a candle, so you have some light," said Koki.

But our fake astrologer did not wait. He crept outside stealthily, trying to see who was making the sounds.

AAAAAH! OWWWWW!

When Koki rushed outside, she saw her husband on the floor. In the pitch black of the night, Goopi had tripped on a stone, and landed hard on the ground.

And guess who was making those scratching sounds? It was not a thief. It was Moti's donkey. He'd followed Moti's scent, and while he was completely lost, he knew his master had been to Goopi's house. He could smell his presence from earlier. He was desperately looking for his master.

On seeing the donkey, Pandit Goopi was delighted. He immediately realised whose

donkey this was. Hearing all the noise, their neighbours came out and asked, "Panditji, what was all the noise about? Are you okay?"

But before he could reply, another neighbour chimed in. "Oh, it's Moti's donkey! You found him using your special powers! So sorry we disturbed you, Panditji. Moti will be overjoyed."

Koki quickly looped a rope around the donkey's

neck and tied him to the porch so that he would not continue on his nightly wanderings. Then she followed Goopi to bed. It had been a very eventful night.

The next morning, Moti was delighted. "Panditji! You are the best astrologer in the world! I knew you would find my donkey and bring him back. Thank you, Panditji!"

Pandit Goopi knew that this was pure luck. But he couldn't say this. He graciously accepted all the praise that Moti lavished on him.

What happened next, though, was very interesting. Our already popular Pandit Goopi now became the most famous astrologer in his village, in the surrounding villages as well and, perhaps, even in the entire kingdom.

This was because Moti did the washing in many villages, and as he went from house to house, he told every person that he met how Panditji, the best astrologer in the world, had found his donkey.

Pandit Goopi became even more sought after; he became even richer. Many months passed, and Goopi's fame and name grew.

A few months later, in King Deviya's palace, there was a loud cry of despair.

OH NOOO!

King Deviya rushed into his daughter's room. "What is the matter, my dear?"

"Father, my favourite pearl necklace, the one you had bought me from your travels to that distant land, is missing. It was my favourite one, father. Someone has stolen it," sobbed Princess Navya.

"Don't worry, my girl. I will find it for you," replied King Deviya.

He immediately summoned the royal guards. "Guards! Send out search parties. Go and

find Princess Navya's necklace. And bring the thief back to me, alive! ALIVE!" he loudly commanded.

"Yes, Sire." They bowed down before him.

But one person, who was at the palace windows, was terrified on hearing these words. It was Chandi, the palace gardener. You see, it was her. She had stolen Princess Navya's pearl necklace.

Her heart was racing. "I had better take this pearl necklace home or maybe even to the next village, before these guards think of searching me," she whispered to herself.

She tucked the necklace into the folds of her sari, pulled her pallu closer and briskly walked away from the palace. She could hear the boots of the guards thumping heavily on the floor, as the royal search started.

By the end of that day, the guards still hadn't found the necklace. King Deviya was furious.

"You are all useless! Summon all the astrologers in the kingdom. They will be able to look into the future and see where the necklace is. We need to find this necklace as soon as possible," yelled King Deviya.

The next morning a band of astrologers stood before King Deviya. "O learned pandits, I have the utmost respect for your powers. I know you will be able to channel your energies and find out where Princess Navya's necklace is. It was stolen from the palace yesterday."

However, the astrologers too were unsuccessful. Princess Navya was heartbroken. She was the apple of King Deviya's eye and the king was not used to not getting his way.

That morning, his favourite courtier bowed down before him. He said, "Your Highness, my cousin lives three villages away from the palace. He told me about the most famous astrologer in the entire kingdom. His name is Pandit Goopi. He is an expert in finding lost things; it is his specialty. With his immense powers he was even able to find the lost donkey of a washerman! Imagine that!"

"Bring him here, immediately!" commanded King Deviya, loudly.

That very evening, Pandit Goopi was brought before King Deviya. "I have heard that you specialise in finding lost things. I heard an incident about a washerman's lost donkey. Princess Navya's precious pearl necklace has been stolen. Panditji, find it in two days and you will be handsomely rewarded," said King Deviya.

Pandit Goopi was terrified. The stakes were higher than ever now.

"I will try my best, Your Highness," he said, bowing down before the king.

"What is this uncertainty? You are supposed to be the best astrologer in the entire kingdom! You better find it in two days, or I will send you to prison," ordered King Deviya. He had been on edge since the robbery of the pearl necklace in his palace.

Pandit Goopi couldn't believe his ears. This wasn't fair. But the king had already dismissed him, with a flick of his wrist.

When Pandit Goopi returned home, he was desperate. He was just a fake astrologer, who had been very lucky. That was the absolute truth of the matter. How on earth was he ever going to find this missing necklace?

He was scared. Not knowing what else to do, he went to the statue of Goddess Chandi and started praying out aloud. "O Goddess! O Chandi! How can I find this necklace? You have to help me now. Save me from prison." He paused, bowed his head down, and then added, "O Chandi, bring me that necklace, now."

Right at that very moment who should be passing by Pandit Goopi's house? The thief herself! Chandi, the palace gardener, had wanted to escape as far as possible from the king and the palace. She had walked from one village to another, and actually was quite tired, hungry and scared. She was also quite lost.

On hearing Pandit Goopi utter these words, she ran into his house and bowed down before him. "Panditji," she cried, "please have mercy on

me. I'm Chandi. I am the gardener in the palace. I'm so sorry. I know that, with your powers, you have discovered my theft. Please, Panditji, please do not reveal my name to King Deviya, or he will have me beheaded."

Pandit Goopi could not believe his good luck.

Here I was calling out to the goddess, and who would have ever dreamt that this foolish girl would have the same name and think that I'm calling out to her, he thought, trying hard not to show his utter delight.

"This is true, Chandi. He will have you killed or, at the very least, throw you in prison," said Pandit Goopi, solemnly. Then he got an idea. "Chandi, is there a pond in the palace?"

"Yes, Panditji. Right at the centre of the palace, near the temple," she replied.

"Here's what we will do. You will put the necklace into a pot, and weigh it down with heavy stones. Then, you will take it to that pond at the centre of the palace, near the temple, and you will drop the pot into the pond. Make sure no one sees you. After that you will lie low and wait. I will tell the king two days after you do this," said Pandit Goopi. "Go, now. Hurry!"

Two days later, Pandit Goopi went to the palace to see the king.

"Have you found my daughter's necklace?" demanded King Deviya.

"Your Highness, give me

just a few minutes and I will tell you exactly where it is," said Pandit Goopi, with a smile.

He proceeded to roll out his mat. Then, as the king watched, he sat cross-legged, back erect, and closed his eyes. He brought his fingertips together, pulled his hands close to his heart and started chanting.

"Findum... searchum... necklace-um... findum..."

Then suddenly, he dramatically opened his eyes. His face seemed to light up. "Your Highness, I can see the necklace!" he exclaimed.

"Where is it, Panditji?" asked the king.

"Your Highness, is there a pond in this palace? Is there any mass of water near here?"

"Yes, Panditji. Right at the centre! We have a pond, right near the temple!" exclaimed the king, looking delighted.

"Your Highness, I can see the necklace. It is in the water in that pond," said Pandit Goopi.

"GUARDS! Dive into the pond. RIGHT NOW! See if what the Panditji says is true!" briskly ordered the king.

In no time at all, one of the guards found the pot in the pond.

"Your Highness, could it be in this?" he asked.

And it was! King Deviya was ecstatic.

"Panditji, thank you for your help. I appoint you as the royal astrologer in my court. I am forever grateful to you. You are truly the best astrologer in the world," declared King Deviya.

Pandit Gopi smiled, and whispered to himself, "And also the luckiest."

The Fox and the Frog

A Folktale from Ladakh

The Zanskar valley in Ladakh is tucked away deep in the Himalayan mountains. It is cold here throughout the year, and the area is full of wild animals. Among them, there once lived a young red fox. His name was Watse.

As winter approached, all the animals started preparing their homes and dens for the bitter cold that had already started to set in. The temperatures had begun to drop, and the

ground was covered with snow. And Watse had a very specific problem.

“Brrrr! It’s such a long way down to Zongla village. I am hungry. I hope I find some food soon,” he said to himself. Watse was slowly making his way down the slopes to the villages.

Momo, the marmot, heard him and scampered out of the way as fast as he could. *Yikes! I had better keep away. I could be his dinner tonight,* thought Momo.

Watse gradually made his way down to the river. As he bent his head to have a large gulp of water, his eye fell on something green. It was a nice, juicy frog. *Hmmm... What's that? That could be dinner,* he thought, with delight.

Watse pounced on the fat frog, and yelled, "Food! And I don't even need to make my way down to Zongla anymore! This is perfect. You've saved me a trip!"

Now this frog's name was Conrad, and he was a clever fellow. He thought, *Humph! Not another*

hungry animal on his way to the village! How many are there? I need to think fast. I can't be this one's dinner!

Right on cue, Watse said, "You look delicious! I've got you, you delicious Froggy!"

"Who are you calling Froggy? I'm Sbal Pa Ring Shing, you silly fox. Put me down right this instant!" commanded Conrad, in a regal tone.

Watse was flustered. "Ummm... What? Huh? W-w-who?" he stammered.

"You ignorant mammal. What's your name? I am the most powerful monk of this century. Haven't you heard of me? You would if you'd keep your nose up and look at the animals around you, instead of downwards – always trying to sniff out your next meal. I am the

MOST POWERFUL monk of this century. I'm just about to attain nirvana. Put me down and begone!" commanded Conrad, in a loud, forceful voice.

Now, Watse had met many wonderful monks during his lifetime. He was really confused and unsure. This had never happened before. *Is he really a monk? Should I let him go?* he thought.

He paused, and then replied, "I'm Watse. You are a frog! If you really are a monk, show me your true form. I need to see it! Not this frog form!"

"Huh? What new nonsense is this? No way! Don't you know? If I do show you my true form, I will lose one hundred years of good karma. I will not waste that on you, Watse," replied Conrad.

Watse couched down and looked ready to pounce. "Grrrr..."

Conrad's heart started racing. Then suddenly, he had the most brilliant idea!

"Watse, relax. Since I am a wise monk, I will give you a solution. Hear me out."

Watse nodded uncertainly. "Go on..."

"It's a simple one. Let's see if you can outjump me. Look at your size, look at mine. Surely, if I am just an ordinary frog, you will not find this hard to do. If you can outjump me, then you can eat me. I will not stop you," replied Conrad, looking him right in the eye.

Watse loved the idea. He was the fox champion in long jump. Whenever he and the other foxes competed, he was miles ahead of them. This was his strength! He couldn't wipe the smile off his face.

"Okay," Watse said. "That sounds like a fair plan. Let's jump across this bend of the river, right here."

"Sure. And to show you just how noble and compassionate I am, I'll let you start ahead of

me. I'll stand here and jump from behind you, Watse," said Conrad. With that, the crafty frog hopped and stood behind the fox.

"Okay! On the count of three?" asked Watse.

"Ready when you are!" cheerfully replied Conrad.

"One, two... and JUMP!" yelled Watse. He just couldn't wait. It was dinner time!

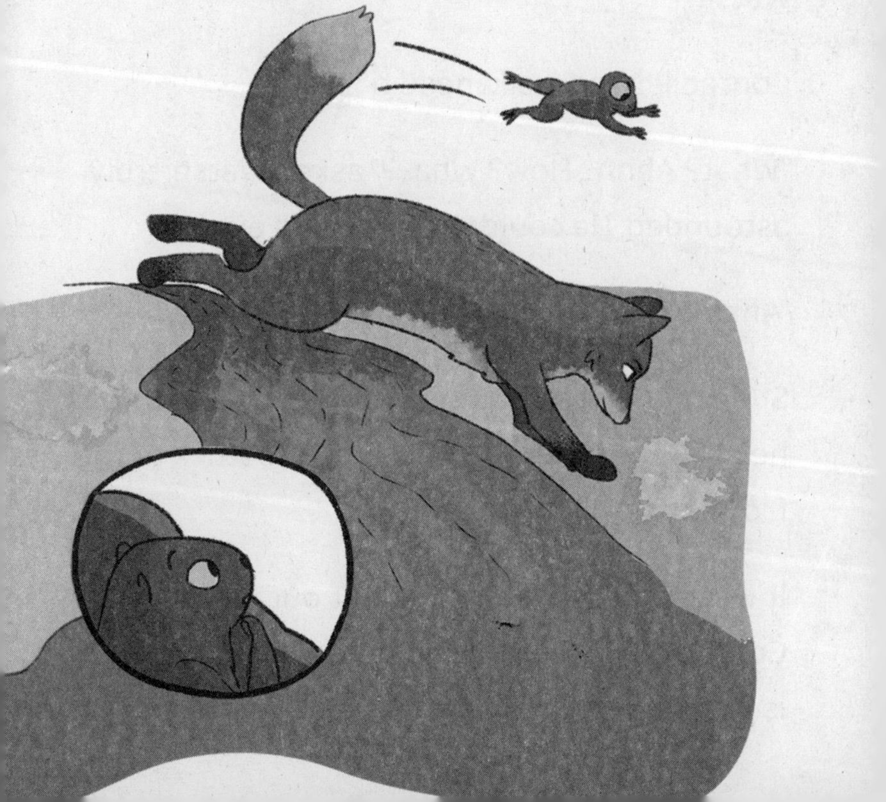

Momo, who happened to be walking by the river, stopped. It was the strangest sight! Right before his eyes, he could see Watse, leaping across the river. But that's not what was weird.

Hanging on to Watse's tail was Conrad! Then, right when Momo thought things couldn't get stranger, he watched as Conrad let go of Watse's tail and leapt ahead... and in FRONT of Watse!

Conrad landed well ahead of Watse.

"What? Ahhh... How? Wha...?" asked Watse, truly astounded. He couldn't believe his eyes.

"Ahem! You were saying?" replied Conrad.

Suddenly, Watse was suspicious. "What is that?" he asked. He had spotted some fur stuck to the frog's sticky webbed feet.

It was actually Watse's fur. But our clever Conrad confidently replied, "Oh, this? This is just some hair off a snow leopard's neck.

He too wouldn't believe that I was the most powerful monk of this century. Hahaha!"

"Snow leopard?" asked Watse, truly alarmed.

This is truly no ordinary frog! If he can pull the fur off a snow leopard, I don't stand a chance, he thought.

"Yes. I sent him to get me my dinner, just before you arrived at the river. I wonder what's taking him so long," replied Conrad, craning his neck to make it seem like he was looking for the snow leopard.

Watse panicked. If there was a snow leopard coming there, he wanted to be far, far away.

"Okay, then. You won fair and square. I'll take your leave, Master Monk," he said, very respectfully.

"Go in peace, little one," replied Conrad, closing his eyes, with a calm, peaceful expression on his face, as if he was a real monk.

And Momo, who had still stuck around to watch how everything would fall in place, chuckled to himself, "I think I'll be safe if I stick close to this clever little frog! If he can outsmart a fox, he can outsmart anyone."

A Love Like Salt

A Folktale from Punjab

King Veerbhadra was a kind and just king. His subjects loved him. He was generous and fair to everyone. Ministers from the neighbouring kingdoms too often visited him to ask for his advice on political issues. He had a sharp mind and was much respected.

He was also wealthy beyond measure. But his biggest treasure was not his money; it was his three daughters – Baani, Ginny and

Janee. They were the apples of his eye. King Veerbhadra would do anything for the three princesses. Their mother, Queen Kastuba, had died a few years before, and Baani, Ginny and Janee were precious to the king. He kept a watchful eye on them.

The three princesses also loved their father very much. They lived a content life in the palace, getting lessons from the royal tutor, eating the wonderful food that the royal chef cooked, playing with their pet rabbit, making tiaras out of the roses from the royal gardens and plucking fruit from the trees. They had each other for company and life was good.

Every year, King Veerbhadra celebrated his birthday with great pomp and splendour. It was the highlight of the entire kingdom's social calendar. It was a much-awaited event. His subjects waited for this yearly event, as the king invited everyone to it.

One year, the day before his birthday, King Veerbhadra had the royal guard bring his three daughters into the court.

"My darlings! How are you? When I got back to the palace last night, it was late and you were all already in bed," said King Veerbhadra, as they walked in.

"We are well, father," said Ginny.

"Are you excited about your birthday, father?" asked Janee.

"Yes, yes, yes," replied the king. "But tell me, my darling daughters, how much do you love me? Baani, you are the eldest, please tell me first."

"Father, what kind of a question really is this? You are the best father in the world. I love you as much as... well, as much as I love gold!" exclaimed Baani.

"Oh, Baani! You are such a lovely daughter. I

am so pleased to hear that. What about you, Ginny?" asked the king, looking towards his second-oldest daughter.

"Father, you are the bravest father that any daughter could ever have. You are both a mother and a father to us. I love you with all my heart. I love you as much as my dazzling diamonds," declared Ginny.

"Oh, my darling! You have filled your old father's heart with such happiness," said the king, smiling from ear to ear.

"And what about you, my youngest love? How much do you love me, Janee?" asked the king, with a twinkle in his eye.

"Father, I love you a lot. I just can't measure my love for you," replied Janee.

"Come now, my child! You must have something to compare it with!" exclaimed the king.

"Well... well, hmmm... I guess I would have to say that I love you like salt, father," said Janee.

"WHAT? Did you just say salt? Did you just compare me to an ordinary, common ingredient like salt? I think it's perhaps the cheapest, most useless ingredient in the kitchen!" roared the king.

"Yes, father. But..."

"Not another word out of you," interrupted the king. "You have humiliated me, Janee. Right here,

in front of everyone. Please leave my court right now. We will talk about this separately, in my royal chambers after I have calmed down."

Janee burst into tears. Sobbing uncontrollably, she ran out of the court and into her room. She had a good, long cry. But as her tears started drying up, she thought, *How can I show father that I love him?*

Janee was an intelligent girl and very soon she got an idea. She ran to the royal kitchen to meet the old chef.

"What brings you to my kitchen, Princess Janee?" asked the royal chef. Of the three princesses, Janee was his favourite. There was nothing he wouldn't do for her.

"Chandu Uncle, I need your help. I need to show father how much I love him. I have a plan, but I need your help," came her reply.

And she whispered her plan into his ear.

The royal chef loved Princess Janee, and he loved her idea. He readily agreed. "Your word is my command, Your Highness," he said, bowing his head.

The sun rose early the next morning. It was the big day – the king's birthday. The guests poured into the palace, dressed in their best silks and finery. The king himself wore his favourite pink kurta and his new jewel-studded royal blue turban with a peacock feather in it.

King Veerbhadra was in a splendid mood. He was laughing and being a gracious host, inviting all his guests to partake in the festivities.

Soon, the royal butler rang a little bell to signify that dinner was served. King Veerbhadra cordially invited the guests to come and sit at the dining table. The guests were looking forward to the feast of their lives. This was the event of the year.

But something was amiss. As each bite was chewed, the whispers grew louder. With each passing minute, voices could be heard...

"It's so bland!"

"It has no taste, no flavour!"

"What's wrong with the food this year?"

The king took a bite of the food served on his plate. The entire spread consisted of all his favourite delicacies. He dipped the roti in the curry served in a round bowl on his plate, and pinched a bit of the potato into it. He put it in his mouth and slowly chewed.

"Argggh! This food is tasteless! Where is the royal chef?" King Veerbhadra was FURIOUS.

The royal chef was immediately summoned from the kitchen. "Chandu! This food is terrible!

This is the royal feast for my birthday. This is the event of the year! What do you have to say for yourself? Why is this food so tasteless?" demanded the king.

"Sire, just yesterday you had said that salt was the most useless ingredient in the kitchen. I was afraid to add this cheap, ordinary ingredient to the food, Sire. Forgive me," said the royal chef, with a tiny bow.

There was a long silence as King Veerbhadra processed this. Then he threw his head back and roared with laughter. "Hahaha. This has got to be my Janee. Janee, my clever girl, you are right! Salt is not useless. It is actually more important than anything in the world. Without salt, our food is tasteless. What can be more precious? Chandu, add some salt to the food this instant!"

"That's right, father," said Janee, not even trying to hide her delight.

"I love you so much, my Janee," said King

Veerbhadra, putting his arms around his youngest daughter and pulling her into a tight hug.

"As much as you love salt, right, father?" asked Janee, cheekily.

"Hahaha, yes. Absolutely," replied the king.

Stars in The Pond

A Folktale from Nagaland

Nagaland, located in North East India, is full of mountains. It is a charming state with breathtaking natural beauty. It is also home to many different tribes. It is popularly known as the 'Land of Festivals', as each of the tribes celebrates their festival in their own particular way, with joy and gusto. Everyone dresses in their most colourful clothes and dances, eats and makes merry. One such tribe, the Angami

Naga tribe, lives in the quaint little village of Khonoma in Nagaland. And this is where our story is set.

Long, long ago, in this tiny village of Khonoma, there lived three brothers – Tanyen, Zhoshu and Penhun. The three might have been brothers, but they could not have been more different from each other. In fact, apart from the same surname, they had barely anything in common.

Tanyen was the eldest of the three. He was smart and hardworking. He looked after his two younger brothers very well.

The second brother was Zhoshu. The only thing he liked to do was daydream and waste his time. Yes, he was very lazy.

The youngest was Penhun. There were only two things that were dear to him. Can you guess what they were? Food and sleep. He was the laziest of the brothers. Even lazier than Zhoshu.

So, as you might imagine, the bulk of the work fell on Tanyen, the eldest brother. He was the one who earned the money, who bought the groceries, who cooked food for all three brothers. He was also the one who cleaned their home. It wasn't fair, but Tanyen was very good-natured about it. He was the eldest, and he took it upon himself to

look after his two younger brothers and help meet their needs as best he could.

One evening, Tanyen had cooked galho, a Naga delicacy, for dinner. It was a soupy, fragrant rice dish, layered with fresh green leaves and vegetables. It was Penhun's favourite dish.

"Guess what's for dinner, my brothers?" asked Tanyen, bringing the pot to the dining space. Zhoshu and Penhun were sitting cross-legged, with their plates set before them, waiting to tuck into the meal.

"My nose says it's galho!" exclaimed Penhun.

"Yes, yes. Your nose is right," said Tanyen.

"Yum. I'm ravenous," said Zhoshu.

Tanyen carefully put the hot pot on the ground, and served his brothers.

But Penhun took one bite of the food on his plate and said, "Ehhh! What is this, brother Tanyen? This doesn't taste right. This doesn't taste at all like galho."

"I know, my brother. Times are hard. I couldn't buy all the spices that I needed to cook it, Penhun. The money that I have earned has run out. I'll try to get another job in the village tomorrow. And after I earn some money, I promise I'll cook it for you again with all the right spices," said Tanyen.

The rest of the dinner was eaten in silence.

You'd think that since Tanyen spelt out that there was no money, his younger brothers would pitch in, right? You'd think they'd help, perhaps they too would get jobs?

But, no.

Despite the shortage of money and the dire situation they were in, the two younger brothers, Zhoshu and Penhun, did nothing to help.

Tanyen chopped the wood for the fireplace in silence. He realised that things could not continue as they were.

The next evening, Tanyen said, "My brothers, we cannot live like this. All our groceries are over. I scraped the last of the lentils and rice from the bottom of the bags today. There is not a single grain of food remaining at home. We have no milk either. Tomorrow I will go from door to door in the village and find myself a job that will earn us more money."

You'd thing that at least NOW the two younger brothers would be ashamed, right?

But, no.

Instead, they had the most absurd reaction to the situation they were all in.

Zhoshu pulled Penhun aside. "I can't believe my ears! Are you thinking what I'm thinking?" asked Zhoshu, his eyebrows raised.

"Yes, I am. Did you notice that there were ingredients missing in tonight's dinner as well? I'm so hungry. What's it going to take to get a decent meal around here?" grumbled Penhun.

"Huh? What are you saying?" asked Zhoshu.

"You asked me what I was thinking, right? That's what I'm thinking," said Penhun.

"No, silly. Stop always thinking about food. Only food! I think Tanyen wants to leave the house, get rich and never return. He wants to leave us to starve here! I think he wants to run away from us," said Zhoshu.

"Oh! Is that so? That would be terrible! What should we do?" asked Penhun.

He was really scared. How would he ever get all the delicious food he needed, if Tanyen didn't cook it for him? His belly wasn't happy with the past few dinners, but he thought that it was only temporary. If Penhun was right, things were going to get much worse. This was a horrible situation.

"Don't worry. I have a plan. I will go and find work in the village tomorrow, instead of Tanyen. And mark my words, I will return with a fortune. We will use the money to buy all the spices, rice, pulses and lentils we need. And we will lead a life fit for kings!" declared Zhoshu.

Penhun looked relieved.

The next morning, Zhoshu rose bright and early. He went to his eldest brother and said, "Brother Tanyen, looking after us shouldn't only be your responsibility. I want to share your burden. I want to pitch in too. You've been looking so stressed out. You stay here at home. Let me go into the village and find a job. I'll earn some

money, and we will be able to buy food with it."

Tanyen was in shock. "This is such a nice change, Zhoshu. My brother, nothing has made me happier than this. This really is music to my ears. Thank you, Zhoshu." Then he embraced his brother, and with tears in his eyes, he added, "May luck favour you, brother Zhoshu."

Zhoshu slowly made his way out. In the village, he went from door to door seeking employment. But it wasn't easy.

At the first house...

"Do you know how to pluck fruit?"

"No," replied Zhoshu, shaking his head.

"Then I'm sorry. There's no work for you here," came the reply.

At the next house...

"Do you know how to weed the garden?"

"No. I do not," replied Zhoshu.

"Then I'm sorry. There's no work for you here," came the reply.

And at the next...

"Do you know how to feed chickens in the coop?"

"No. I don't think I do," replied Zhoshu, looking down at his feet.

"Then I'm sorry. There's no work for you here," came the reply.

On and on it went.
And poor Zhoshu was exhausted. One hour merged into the next, and

he had absolutely no luck with finding a job... Till he knocked on the door of a very old woman.

"Excuse me, aunty. Do you think you can give me some food and shelter for tonight? I'm a very long way from home. I've been going from door to door looking for a job, as times are hard for me and my two brothers. But I've not been lucky. I'm too far away from home to make my way back tonight. I need a place to sleep," said Zhoshu.

"Come in, son. Come in," replied the old woman. Then she looked him in the eye and said, "Actually, I have a job for a young, strapping man like you. Come to my backyard."

The old woman took Zhoshu through her living room and kitchen and into her backyard. There, right in the middle, was a small, perfectly round pond. "Here. This right here is my problem," she said, pointing towards the pond.

"The pond? I don't understand," said Zhoshu.

"Look child, LOOK! Can you not see the stars in this pond? They dazzle like diamonds. It is too much to handle for these old eyes that have already seen too much in this world. Remove these stars, young man, and I will pay you handsomely," said the old woman, with a sharp tilt of her head.

Zhoshu gave up without even trying.

How can I possibly remove the stars from this pond? The water on the pond's surface is just reflecting the stars in the sky. What is this

woman talking about? She must not be sane, he thought.

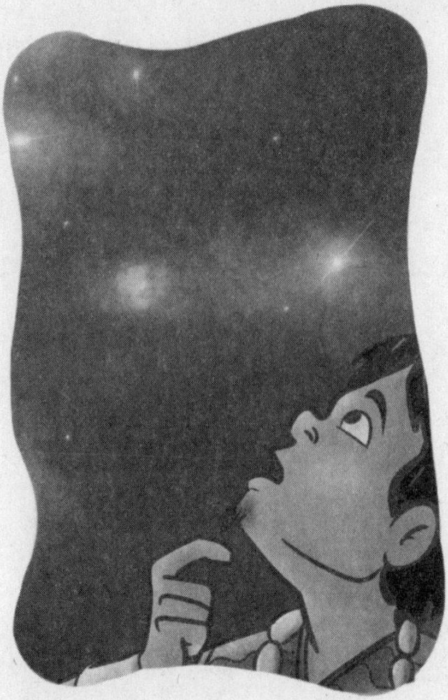

"Aunty, you have a very weird request," he said.

"Weird? How so?" asked the old woman.

"I don't think anyone can solve your problem, aunty," replied Zhoshu.

"Is that so? Hmmm... that remains to be seen, young man. If you cannot solve my problem, you cannot stay here. It's as simple as that. So, you must go now," she replied, icily.

Poor Zhoshu dragged his feet and trudged out. He walked for a few miles, but was too tired to walk further. He found a rock to use as a pillow, lay down on the grass and fell asleep.

As the sun rose, the fierce rays fell on him, and woke him up. His back ached and his bones felt frozen from sleeping outside. He realised that he was hungry and tired. He missed the comfort of his home. He slowly stood up,

stretched his body, dusted his clothes and started on the long walk back home, with nothing to show for his efforts.

Zhoshu reached home, tired and weary. Every bone in his body ached. He was starving. He hadn't eaten a decent meal in hours.

Tanyen ran to meet him. Zhoshu took one look at his anxious face, and he knew what his unasked question was. "Oh, brother Tanyen. I failed. I failed to find work, and I failed to find my fortune. I'm sor-sor-sorry," he stammered, blinking back the tears in his eyes.

"Brother Zhoshu, don't lose heart. You tried. Things will work out, don't worry. Go and wash yourself, lie down on the mattress and rest for a while. You look exhausted. I will go and cook some food for you," said Tanyen.

As Tanyen was in the kitchen, looking at what to make from nothing, Penhun walked in. Tanyen quickly whispered to him about

Zhoshu's unsuccessful trip.

"What do you think we should do next, brother Penhun?" asked Tanyen.

There was a small pause. Then Penhun replied, "Don't worry about it, brother Tanyen. I will go! Allow me to go and seek my fortune."

Tanyen couldn't believe his ears! His youngest brother was being mature and responsible and stepping up to the plate!

"I'm so proud of you, Penhun!" he said, as he embraced him. "May luck favour you, my brother."

Penhun quickly packed a few of his belongings into a sack, threw it over his shoulder and left home, with a spring in his step.

Without knowing it, Penhun followed the same path as his brother Zhoshu. And just like Zhoshu he received the reply...

"Then I'm sorry. There's no work for you here."

... over and over again. He looked for work, in vain, for three full days. He was tired, hungry and disheartened. He had survived on food that kind strangers had shared with him.

He walked towards the last house that he could see, for that night. He knocked on the door. And guess whose home it was! Yes, the same old woman that Zhoshu had visited a few nights earlier.

The old woman opened the door.

"Aunty, may I get some food? I'm so tired and hungry. I could do some work for you in return," he said, wearily.

"Actually, I do have a problem. I need help with one big thing. If you can do that, I will provide you with food and shelter for tonight. And I will pay you handsomely," replied the old woman, with a small smile.

The old woman took Penhun through her living room and kitchen and into her back yard.

Pointing at the, round pond, she said, "Here. This right here is my problem. Take out these stars from my pond!"

Penhun was foxed. Then he thought to himself, *This is a huge task. If I have to make the stars disappear from this pond, I'll need to find a ladder that is long enough to reach the sky. It will need to have at least two thousand steps! Maybe more! I'm too tired for this job. It is too much work for my exhausted, starving body.*

"Aunty, I'm so sorry. I don't think it is possible for anyone to take out the stars from this pond. No one can do this work for you. I guess I will have to go find work and some food and shelter elsewhere," said Penhun, as he showed himself out of her house.

He paused once he was outside and considered his options. And then he realised that he actually only had one option before him – to return home to Tanyen and Zhoshu.

It was a very long walk home, but eventually Penhun made it. Both his brothers greeted him joyfully, only to later find out that he had been unsuccessful too. Tanyen then took matters into his own hands.

The next morning, he packed a few of his belongings into a sack, and set out for the village to look for work.

Like both his brothers had done before him, he knocked on one door after the next, till eventually, he too landed at the same old woman's house.

The old woman opened the door and asked him, "Are you looking for work?"

Tanyen was surprised. "Yes, I am, aunty. How did you know?" he asked.

"Well, twice, two different young men also came by looking for a job. But they were both lazy and not too bright. I don't want to waste my time with you if you are not interested," said the old woman, grumpily.

"Oh, aunty! Those might have been my

brothers. Please give me a chance. I really need to earn some money. What is your work?" he asked.

"Fine." She took Tanyen through her living room and kitchen and into her backyard. "I will give you the same task that I gave them. Remove the stars from the pond in my backyard, and I will pay you handsomely," she said.

Tanyen took one look at the pond and thought, *This is an easy task!*

"Aunty, please give me three hours. When you come back, you won't find a single star in your pond. I promise," said Tanyen.

"Very well," she replied, with a nod of her head. "Take your time."

Tanyen set to work. He quickly picked a bucket from the garden shed and started emptying the water from the pond into the surrounding garden. Bucket after bucket after bucket...

SPLISH! SPLASH! SPLOSH!

Three hours later, there was not a drop of water in the pond.

The old woman came out to the backyard. Tanyen pointed at the empty pond and said,

"See? All the stars are gone!"

The old woman was delighted. "You are a smart young man. You are hardworking and you used your wit! Come into my home, rest and eat the hot dinner that I have prepared for you."

"Thank you, aunty," said Tanyen.

The next morning, when Tanyen woke up, the old woman said to him, "Young man, I am going to live with my daughter in the next village. I am too old to look after all this land, my fields and my crops. I am gifting all of this, and also this house, my home, to you. Work hard and look after it well. This is all yours now. I told you I would pay you handsomely."

Tanyen couldn't believe his ears!

He spent the next several months tilling the fields, sowing the seeds, harvesting and selling

the crops. Then he returned home with his pockets jingling with money, and brought his brothers back with him to help him in the fields.

Zhoshu and Penhun also learnt to work hard, in time. Money was never short for the rest of their days.

FUNNY FOLKTALES

WRITTEN BY

CHRISTOPHER BARETTO

ILLUSTRATED BY

BHAVYA KUNTAL DESAI

The Crow, The Deer and The Jackal

Long ago, there lived a deer and a crow. They were best friends and loved each other dearly. They would go on all sorts of adventures together. They shared their meals and defended each other in times of need. They were inseparable.

One day, a jackal saw the deer. He thought to himself, "That's a delicious looking deer. I can feast on him!"

Without a second thought, he went up to the deer and said to him, "Good day, my friend." The deer was startled. He said, "Wh-ho are you?"

"I am a lonely jackal. I wander from forest to forest. I have no friends. But now that I have met you, you will be my friend, right?" said the jackal. The deer was pure-hearted. He didn't see prey or predator in any animal. He whole-heartedly accepted the jackal's friendship.

The deer decided to introduce the jackal to his friend, the crow. The crow was smart. He said, "My dear friend, you should be careful of who you choose to be friends with. Being friends with an absolute stranger is not a good idea."

Upon hearing this, the jackal knew that he couldn't let his meal go away

so easily. He decided to reason with the crow. He said, "Dear sir, you seem to forget that the first time you met this deer, you too were a stranger. But look at you two now! Your friendship only grows stronger by the day. How about you and I become friends as well?"

While this heated debate was on, the deer took it upon himself to calm everyone down. He said to the crow, "Come on, my friend. Let us all live together in harmony." Finally, the crow had no other option but to agree and accept the jackal's friendship. And so, the three became friends.

Soon, the three of them began living together. They would wake up early in the morning and set out in search of food and return late at night. At night, they would share stories about their day, laugh and have a good time.

One morning, after the crow had left in search of his food, the jackal went to the deer and said, "Friend, in the depths of this forest, there is an area where the world's sweetest grain grows. Allow me to escort you to that field." Without having second thoughts, the deer followed his friend to the field.

The deer enjoyed grazing in the field. He said to the jackal, "You were absolutely right, my friend! This is indeed the sweetest grain in the world. I shall come here every day and feast on it." The cunning jackal thought to himself, "Yes,

yes. Feed on it. Soon, you'll be plump and then I shall feed on you."

The duo visited the field regularly. The deer would graze in the field and the jackal would patiently hide in a bush and wait. One day, the farmer who owned the field happened to notice the deer. He then set up a snare to catch the thief. Things were going exactly as the jackal had hoped. Soon, the farmer caught the deer.

HEEEEEEEEEEEEEELP MEEEEEEEEEEEEE!

The deer began crying for help. But there was no one to hear him. No one except the jackal. The jackal sprung out

of the bush, laughed and said to himself, "Aha! My time has finally come! All those days of pretending to be this deer's friend have finally borne fruit. Once the farmer cuts him up, his bones, gristle

and blood will make for an extremely delicious meal."

When the deer saw his friend, the jackal, approaching, he was relieved. He said, "Friend, you are just in time! Gnaw at this net and save me!"

The evil jackal refused. "I'm sorry my friend, the material with which this net is made is too strong for me. I cannot help you," he said, and left.

When the crow returned home that night, he noticed that both the jackal and the deer were missing. He had never trusted the jackal. Fearing the worst, he immediately began worrying for his friend. He went out to look for him.

After searching for hours, the crow finally found the deer trapped in the net. The deer told him everything that had happened and how the jackal refused to help him. "The traitor! I knew it! Where

is that sly jackal now?" asked the crow.

"He must be hiding in the bushes, waiting for me to be killed by the farmer," said the deer. The deer insisted that the crow escape lest he also fall in the trap. However, the crow was the deer's true friend. He began racking his brains, thinking of a way to save his friend.

AHA!

Suddenly, an idea popped into the crow's head. He said to the deer, "Now do exactly as I say. Lie on your back, puff out your stomach, stiffen your legs and be extremely still. I will come and pretend to pluck out your eyes. As soon as I croak, spring up and run as fast as you can. Understood?" The deer nodded.

Soon, the farmer came there. He had a club in his hand to kill the deer. But when he saw the deer, he assumed that he had already died. "That just makes things easier for me," he said to himself. The farmer began to remove the net from the deer's body. As he was busy folding the net...

CROAAAAAAAAAK!
CROAAAAAAAAAK!
CROAAAAAAAAAK!

The deer remembered the crow's instructions and ran as fast as he could. He had managed to escape! Upon seeing this, the jackal frowned. The farmer was furious. He threw his club in a fit of rage. The club went and hit the jackal who instantly died on the spot.

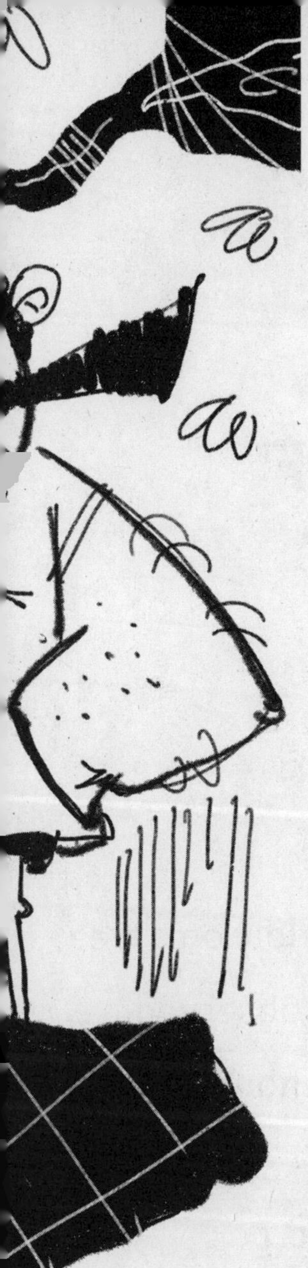

From that day onwards, the deer became more careful of whom he trusted and befriended. However, the deer knew that he could always trust the crow to be his true friend.

CHOICE OF FRIENDS

One day, a crow was sitting idly on a tree near the Godavari river. He observed a hunter approaching and thought to himself, "Oh dear! This man is clearly up to no good. I wonder what he is doing."

The hunter started hiding a net cleverly behind some bushes. He then sprinkled some grains on the ground and hid inside one of the hollow trees and waited patiently.

A couple of pigeons accompanied by their king were flying by. One of the pigeons saw the grains and said, "Your Majesty, look! There are some grains on the ground. Let us rest and feed on them."

The king said, "Hold on. Isn't it a bit odd that there are grains spread over here, in the middle of the forest?" The crow heard that and thought, "This king is wise."

The Pigeon King continued, "We must be cautious, for greed will lead one to great doom." All the other pigeons agreed except for one. He said, "Should we give up a feast for an irrational fear?" Suddenly, the other pigeons were confused. They didn't know whom to support. One of them agreed with the pigeon and said, "Yes, Your Majesty, he

is right. Let us not be scared out of a good meal." One by one, all the pigeons agreed and decided to eat the grains. All but the king.

The king said to himself, "They are my subjects. I mustn't abandon them." The crow knew that this was a bad idea but couldn't do anything about it.

As soon as the pigeons started pecking at the grain, a giant net trapped them all. They all screamed for help and then looked directly at the pigeon that had suggested pecking the grains in the first place. They said, "Fool! It is because of your greed that we're trapped here. The king was right! We should've listened to him."

The king then hushed the entire flock of pigeons and said, "He isn't the only one to blame. You were ready to share the feast, now be ready to share the blame too! Now let's figure out a way to free ourselves."

The crow thought to himself, "Spoken like a true king."

The Pigeon King then thought of a plan. He instructed all of the other pigeons to fly upwards at the same time. On his mark, they did exactly as instructed by their king and the entire flock of pigeons flew up in the sky along with

the net. The crow decided to follow the pigeons.

Now that the pigeons were safe from the hunter, they had to get themselves out of the net. The Pigeon King had a friend who was king of the mice. The king knew that his friend would be able to gnaw at the net and free him and his subjects. So, he led the flock to his burrow.

At his burrow, the king called out to the mouse. "O friend, please come out and help us!" As soon as the mouse heard that sound, he knew it was his friend. He immediately came out of his burrow to find his friend in an unfortunate

situation. Without a word, he rushed towards the net to gnaw at the strings and free all the pigeons.

"Hold on!" said the Pigeon King, "Free my

followers first."

"But my friend, I am just a tiny creature. It might be possible that my strength fails me before I free you," replied the mouse. The noble Pigeon King replied, "As a king, it is my duty to protect my subjects even if it has to be at the cost of my life."

But, the mouse hesitated. He said, "Absolutely not! I will first save you and then save your subjects. It isn't wise to sacrifice oneself to preserve one's dependents." The Pigeon King smiled gently and replied, "That may be true, my friend. But, death, which comes to all, comes nobly when we give our life

to save another's life. You will free them first." The crow, who was observing all of this at a distance, couldn't believe the nobility of this king.

The mouse finally agreed and began gnawing the net. One by one, all the pigeons escaped. However, it looked like the mouse was running out of

strength. Things seemed desperate but the mouse held on and managed to free every single pigeon, including the king. The pigeons rejoiced. The crow thought to himself, "He is indeed a true friend. I must befriend him."

Once the pigeons flew away, the crow went up to the mouse and told him that he wished to befriend him. The mouse was amused to hear that. The mouse is usually food to the crow. He told him, "We can never be friends! One day, I might end up becoming your dinner." The crow laughed and said, "Oh, you mustn't worry about that. You are too tiny to even be a full breakfast for me."

The mouse was still not sure about this offer. He said to the crow, "But you are so flighty! How can I depend on you?" The crow was keen on being friends

with the mouse. So, he said to him, "Dear mouse, I value your friendship and thus if you refuse it, I will fast unto death at your door."

The mouse was absolutely touched by the crow's gesture and sheer devotion. He decided to become friends with him. He said to the crow, "Come, my friend, let us mark this new friendship with a feast!" And so, from that day onwards, the crow and the mouse became the best of friends. They helped each other with food while staying loyal to each other.

One day, the crow came to the mouse with some unfortunate news. He told him that he would have to leave the forest as the food was getting scarce for him. There was a tortoise in another forest who was his friend and would provide him with fish and other food.

The mouse had come to adore the crow. He couldn't imagine his life without his friend. So, he decided to join him too. The duo left for the other forest to meet the crow's friend, the tortoise. They soon

met him there and the three became the best of friends. They enjoyed each other's company.

Several days passed. The trio was relaxing in the forest when a deer sprang up

to them and said, "Help me! A hunter is after me!"

"Relax and enjoy some food and beverages. I am going for a swim," said the tortoise.

The deer was getting restless. He advised the crow and the mouse to leave the forest immediately. They both agreed. However, they had to figure out a way to take their friend, the tortoise, along with them. Just then...

AHHHHHHHHHHHHHHHHHH!

The crow, the mouse and the deer heard a familiar sound. It was the tortoise. He had been captured by the hunter. The trio had to rescue their friend somehow. The mouse came up with an idea. He instructed the deer to lie across the hunter's path as if he were dead. He asked the crow to then peck at the deer's body. The two

immediately took their positions.

As the hunter was walking with his catch, he saw a dead deer and a crow pecking at him. He put the tortoise down, removed his knife and slowly proceeded towards the deer. The mouse then sneakily began gnawing at the binding strings that imprisoned the tortoise and freed him.

Meanwhile, the hunter was about to skin the deer when...

BOING!

The deer sprang up and ran for his life. The hunter was disappointed but he knew that at least he had the tortoise.

However, he got the shock of his life when he looked back to see that the tortoise had vanished! The hunter's greed had got the better of him. He went back to his hut.

The tortoise thanked the deer, the mouse and the crow for saving him and the four of them enjoyed the rest of their days together.

Bikal The Terrible

Once there was a tiger who lived in a forest. He would often wander in the village nearby. The villagers were aware of this fact and thought it was best to stay indoors at night. On most nights, the tiger would just peacefully stroll around before going back to the forest.

One night, as the tiger was prowling outside a merchant's house, he overheard two people talking. The first voice said, "I'm going out." The second voice replied, "At this hour? Are you crazy? Aren't you afraid of Bikal? When Bikal is out there, even the bravest men do not dare to go out of their houses."

Bikal is a word that means something which is to be feared. In this case, it was the tiger.

However, the tiger wasn't aware of this fact. He thought about this Bikal and started imagining all sorts of things. His own thoughts and overthinking made him fear Bikal. He knew that he had to hide somewhere. He decided to hole up in a nearby shed.

Later that night, a couple of thieves broke into the merchant's house and stole nearly two tonnes worth of money and jewellery. They couldn't carry everything at once and needed a cart. They spotted the shed in which the tiger was hiding and decided to look for a cart over there.

It was pitch dark so the thieves assumed that the resting tiger was actually a bullock. They couldn't find a cart so they decided to put their sacks of loot on the tiger's back. While they talked, the tiger was fast asleep.

Even in his dreams, he was haunted by Bikal.

He began shouting in his dreams, "Help! Help! Bikal has caught me by the tail!" Little did he know that it was actually one of the thieves. The tiger instantly woke up. He found himself being loaded and burdened with heavy sacks. The tiger thought to himself, "I am a ferocious tiger. No one would dare come near me. My worst fears have come true. Bikal and his friends have gotten hold of me."

The thieves were pulling the tiger assuming it was a bullock and the tiger didn't protest, assuming he was being pulled by none other than Bikal. The tiger feared for his life.

At dawn, the thieves decided to check the loot since they were now able to see better. When they turned back to check the loot, they screamed...

TIGEEEEEEEEEEEEEEEEEEER!

The thieves ran for their lives, leaving the loot on the tiger's back. The tiger realised what a fool he was. He thought to himself, "Everyone will laugh at me if they find out about this. I must let this remain a secret."

As he was wandering about in the forest with a heavy sack on his back, he got stuck between two rocks. There was no way he could get out of this situation. He then noticed a cowherd and called out to him. As soon as the cowherd saw the tiger, he decided to run for it. The tiger then shouted, "Don't run away! Help me get this sack off my back. It is

full of money. You can have all of it!"

As soon as the cowherd heard the word 'money', he turned back and decided to help the tiger. Soon, he managed to get the sacks off the tiger's back.

He then asked the tiger, "How did this happen?" To which, the tiger replied, "It's all because of that Bikal." The cowherd was shocked, for the tiger was Bikal. The tiger warned the cowherd to never utter that word ever again. "If I ever find out that you have uttered that word, I will find you and devour you. Understood?" The cowherd agreed and ran back to his house.

Overnight, the cowherd became a rich man. With his newfound wealth, he bought a lot of cattle and became really successful. He married a beautiful woman and started his own family.

One day, his wife asked him, "Dear, how did you become so rich?" The cowherd

replied, "You see, there was this tiger, his name was Bikal..." and began narrating the entire incident.

That very night, the tiger decided to go and meet the cowherd who had helped him. When he went to his house, he overheard him utter the forbidden word. The tiger decided to devour him.

Later that night, when the cowherd went to sleep, the tiger went inside his house, stealthily dragged the cowherd and left. He carried the cowherd deep into the forest and then...

THUD!

He dropped the cowherd on the ground.

The cowherd immediately woke up. He was confused. The tiger said, "You have broken your promise. I will eat you now!"

"WAIT!" said the cowherd, "If you must

eat me then I suggest you eat me in the morning as my flesh will be cold and difficult to chew at night." The tiger agreed and waited patiently for sunrise.

Meanwhile, the cowherd's wife noticed his absence. She saw the tiger's footprints and understood what had happened. She followed the footprints all the way to the jungle.

Sometime later, the tiger who was waiting for sunrise heard an unusual sound.

DHOOM CHANANANANANAN DHAM!

CHOOM CHOOM CHOOM!

TAK TAK TAK TAK TAK!

"What's that?" said the tiger. The cowherd understood from the sound of anklets that it was his wife coming to rescue him. The tiger asked the question again, "I asked you something. What is that?! Is that Bikal?" To let his wife know his position, the cowherd screamed at the top of his lungs...

YES! IT IS BIKAL!

His wife received the signal. She followed the sound and found her husband with the tiger. She understood that the tiger thought that she was Bikal. So, she decided to play upon that.

She changed her voice and said, "WHO'S THERE?! ARE THERE ANY TIGERS AROUND FOR ME TO EAT?

AHA! I CAN SMELL A TIGER!"

The tiger was now afraid. He asked the cowherd to save him. The cowherd asked the tiger to lie down with his face on the ground.

The voice then said, "SPEAK UP!

HAVE YOU SEEN ANY TIGERS AROUND?"

The cowherd replied, "No, I haven't.

Now go away."

"WHAT'S THAT NEXT TO YOU?!"

"This? Oh, it's just a pile of dirty clothes."

"REALLY? I DON'T BELIEVE YOU! HIT IT WITH A ROCK."

At first the cowherd hesitated. But, the tiger gave him the permission to do so. Even then, the cowherd hit him very gently. The voice said, "HARDER!" and so the cowherd did exactly that.

This went on for a while. The voice kept saying "harder" and the cowherd kept hitting the tiger until he finally fainted.

The clever couple left the tiger to its fate and returned home happily. They swore to never utter the forbidden word ever again.

Palita and Lomasha

In the depths of a forest, there was a large banyan tree. It was the largest banyan tree in the forest. At the foot of this tree, there was a small hole. A tiny rat named Palita lived there. Palita was a timid yet smart rat.

On the branches of the same tree, there lived a cat named Lomasha. Palita was in constant fear of him. Every day, Palita would see Lomasha devour an innocent

bird and think to herself, "I must hide in here for as long as possible and be very careful or else one day that could be me." Palita would look for an opening to get out of the hole.

Some days, she would get an opening when Lomasha was busy devouring a bird that he had caught or when he was napping after a meal. This became a daily routine for Palita.

One day, a hunter decided to enter the forest. He knew that this territory was untouched. Every day he would place a trap in the morning and come back in the evening to find an animal trapped in there. He was having the time of his life. Lomasha noticed this hunter and his patterns and tried to keep as far away from him as possible. However, one day...

MEOOOOOOOOOOOOOW!

Lomasha screamed, for it was he who had got trapped in the hunter's net. He tried to use his claws to get out but it was of no use. He jumped around and rolled to get the net off him but it only made things worse. Hope was dwindling for Lomasha.

At that moment, Palita saw Lomasha struggling. She began dancing with joy. "My arch-enemy has finally been caught! I can roam about freely now!" she said to herself. Now that Lomasha was entrapped in a net, the timid Palita

became extremely bold.

She went to Lomasha and said, "My dear Lomasha, you have no idea how happy I am right now! With you being trapped like this, all my dreams have finally come true." Lomasha stared at the rat helplessly.

As Palita was dancing, she noticed some rustling in the bushes. With a keener glance, she could make out that a MONGOOSE was hiding in the bushes! It was waiting for the right time to pounce on Palita and eat her. Palita's happiness was short-lived.

Before Palita could think of a way to avoid the mongoose, she looked up at the banyan tree's branch to find an owl quietly staring at her. Palita only became more nervous.

She didn't know what to do. Danger had surrounded her from all sides. If she

tried to run away, the mongoose would tear her up. However, if she decided to stay there, the owl would swoop down and catch her.

At that moment, Palita learned quite

a valuable lesson. She realised that in a way, Lomasha was protecting her from threats such as these which were far worse. But what could she do about it now? She thought for a while and said to herself, "I should help Lomasha escape this net. That way, he can continue to protect me from these dangers. He needs me and I need him."

Palita approached Lomasha. She had a completely different attitude this time. She smiled and said, "Dear Lomasha, we can be of help to each other. I will help you get out of this trap if you agree to help me."

Lomasha was confused. He said to her, "Help you?! Do you think I will believe in such nonsense? A few minutes ago you were dancing at my misfortune!" Palita

replied, "Things are different now. I have realised that I have a greater enemy. Look around, there's the mongoose and then if you look up, you'll find the owl."

Lomasha looked around and saw both the predators waiting for their chance. He looked at Palita and said, "All right. I will help you. But how can I do anything while being entrapped?" Palita replied, "Let me

hide under your body until they leave."

The cat agreed and Palita crouched under his body.

It was an unusual sight. A rat and a cat working together. The mongoose saw the duo and said, "I can't believe this! However, I also cannot wait forever for the rat to come out. Otherwise, I will end up starving. Might as well find another prey." The mongoose quietly left. However, the owl stayed for a little longer.

After growing impatient with waiting, the owl looked at the duo and said, "I cannot wait forever. It will soon be daybreak.

I must leave and find another prey," and flew away. Palita's plan had worked! Now that both the threats had gone away, it was safe for her to come out of hiding.

It was now time for Palita to keep her side of the bargain. She immediately began gnawing through the net. However, she had something else in mind. She was purposely biting slowly. Lomasha said, "Hurry up! The hunter will come anytime now." Palita replied, "Don't you worry. Patience is the key," and continued gnawing through the net.

Lomasha was trembling with fear at the thought of the hunter devouring him. Meanwhile, Palita knew not to trust the cat. There could be a high chance that he might eat her the second she freed him.

Soon, the sun rose and both Lomasha and Palita could see the hunter approaching. At that very moment, Palita cut the last few strings of Lomasha's net. As soon as she was done, she ran back inside her hole. Lomasha, too, bolted away.

When the hunter arrived at the scene, he was shocked to see that the net had been torn into bits and pieces. When he left, Lomasha addressed his new friend. He said, "Dear Palita, thank you so much for saving my life. Let there be peace between us always. I shall ask all my friends to not hurt you." Upon hearing this, the wise Palita said, "No my dear friend, you are mistaken. My self-interest got the better of me and made me help you out in a desperate moment. Sooner or later, we are bound to be enemies. It could also be possible that

you are pretending to be my friend so that it's easier for you to catch me."

"You are mistaken." said Lomasha. However, Palita had made up her mind. She said, "Let us part ways, Lomasha. Be sure to stay away from the evil hunter."

The moment Lomasha heard that word, his spine shivered. He sprang up and ran for his life. Palita never saw him again.

The Swan and the Crow

Once, there was a crow that lived by a beach. This crow was slightly different from others as he had three admirers. These were three little kids who had a weird obsession with this one particular crow. Every day, they would bring him

some leftover food to eat.

"Come, come, lovely crow! We won't hurt you!" they would scream at the crow in an attempt to lure him towards the food. The crow didn't sense any harm from the kids and landed near the food and ate it peacefully. This was no regular meal for the crow. For when he ate, the kids would shower him with praises.

"What a lovely crow!"

"Look at his wings. They're so glossy."

"This crow is so classy!"

The constant admiration from the kids filled the crow with pride. It made him believe that he was the most handsome and the cleverest bird in the world. His peers warned him that pride to a certain extent is good for one's self-esteem but anything more would only bring his

downfall. However, the crow paid no attention to his peers' words and flew off to the skies.

One day, the crow spotted a bevy of swans. These swans were magnificent and flew with flair and finesse. Anyone who saw these swans would stare for hours in awe, admiring their beauty.

However, at the sight of these swans, the crow was completely irritated. He screamed at the swans, "Listen here, you strangers! This is my beach and I won't tolerate any ugly birds in my territory. Leave at once!"

Upon hearing the crow, the leader of

the swans glided down and said to him, "Ugly? Kind sir, you must be severely mistaken. Everyone knows that a swan's beauty is unparalleled."

Other swans whispered amongst each other. They wondered if the crow was actually addressing himself with these remarks. Lucky for them, the crow didn't hear that.

"I am very well aware of what I'm saying," said the crow, "now fly away like you would, in a disgusting manner." The leader of the swans was extremely patient. He said, "Again, you must be mistaken, sir. We, swans, are the world's best fliers."

Upon hearing this, the crow laughed.

He said, "That's absolutely ridiculous! All you can do is flutter in the breeze like a torn ribbon. I've seen paper fly more elegantly than you. Whereas, look what I can do as a flier..."

And so, the crow lifted himself up and began showing the swans all sorts of tricks. He made several spiral and zig-zag patterns in the air. They were perfectly coordinated and timed for him to put on a marvellous show. It

was as if the swans were watching a professional acrobat.

For a while, the crow even flew upside down. He followed this up by flying at a high speed, sometimes just grazing past the swans to startle them.

However, the swans knew better. They were barely impressed by the crow's parlour tricks. The leader of the swans said to the bevy, "What a clumsy fool he is."

Soon, the crow made a perfect landing. Any other animal or human would have applauded but the swans were least interested. One of the swans said, "Those are just tricks! Any circus clown could do them!" The crow was offended. He said, "Is that so? Why don't you do them and show us?"

However, the swans knew better than

to stoop to the crow's level. One of the swans said to the crow, "We know only one kind of flying and in fact, I can beat you at that!"

The crow was all fired up. He said to the swan, "All right then, state your terms!" The swan said, "Oh, it's simple. We shall fly across the ocean. Whoever successfully manages to do that is the winner." The crow didn't pay any attention to what the swan was saying. He only thought about how effortlessly he was going to beat the swan.

Soon, both the birds took their positions and at the other swan's signal, they flew.

At first, the crow gained speed. "I need to finish this race as quickly as possible. I have other important things to do, you see," said the crow. However, he began to slow down gradually. That's when the swan gained speed and height. In no time, the swan was able to glide over the ocean effortlessly.

The crow knew that he couldn't give up so easily. He decided to gather all the energy he had in himself and blasted off ahead. He managed to overtake the swan but only for a couple of seconds. With every flap of his wings, the crow grew more tired and eventually, he was completely drained. He needed a place to rest for a while. However, he was entirely surrounded by the ocean.

He thought to himself, "What shall I do?! There's no tree or land in sight. Where can I stop to rest? If I don't stop, I'll fall into the ocean and drown." The walls were closing in on the crow and soon he saw himself descend slowly towards the ocean. He tried flapping his wings as much as possible to stay above the water. He then started screaming, "HELP! HELP! Somebody save me or else I'll drown!"

At that moment, the swan returned. He said, "What kind of flying is that, my kind friend? Your beak and wings seem to be constantly touching the water." The crow could tell a taunt when he heard one. He said to the swan, "Now is not the time for taunting me. I am exhausted. In a few minutes, I will drown and die."

The swan took pity on the crow and allowed him to rest on his back. He then flew the crow to the seashore. Then, he placed the crow gently on the sand.

The crow had learnt his lesson. He said to the leader of the swans, "Brother, I have been a fool. You are clearly the superior bird. Prosperity makes foolish ones more foolish. I am indeed only a crow. Thank you for putting me in my place."

The swans smiled at the crow and flew away!

THE QUICK-WITTED FROG

It was a bright, sunny day. Flowers danced in the sunlight and butterflies swayed with joy. Amidst this happiness, a frog decided to jump out of his pond to take a look at the world around him and bask in nature's glory.

He admired the beautiful day and began hopping around bushes and trees. As he was hopping around...

CLANK!

Suddenly, he found himself in the grip of a claw. Soon, the frog saw himself moving farther away from the ground. He thought the world looked much

more beautiful now. He then looked back to find that he had been grabbed by his enemy, a crow. "Aha! After all those years of chasing you, I have finally caught hold of you. Now, I shall feast on you!" said the crow.

The frog was worried. He had to do

something and get out of the crow's clutches before he was devoured. He thought to himself, "What can I do? I will certainly die! But then again, if death is a certainty, what can I gain by giving way to despair?" With that, he decided to do something about his situation.

The crow placed the frog on the top of a hill. Just then...

HAHAHAHAHAHAHA!

The frog began laughing. The crow was confused. He said to him, "You fool! You are about to die and you laugh? Do you not fear death?" The cheerful frog took a pause between his laughs and said, "It is you who should be fearing death, my friend. Look around you! You're in more danger than I am. We are in the snake's natural habitat. The one who lives here will be sure to eat you."

Without a second thought, the crow picked up the frog and flew away from the hilltop. He had the frog in his beak.

Soon, he landed on a tree and placed the frog on a branch. The frog looked around for a while and then...

HAHAHAHAHAHAHA!

"What is it now?" asked the crow, "There are no snakes to be found on this tree. So then why are you laughing?"

The frog replied, "You're right. There are no snakes here. But, what are you going to do about the cat that lives on this tree? In fact, she is right behind you, looking for the right moment to pounce at you."

The crow knew about this cat and didn't want to take any chances. So,

without further ado, the crow grabbed the frog and blasted off into the sky, looking for another place to feast on the frog.

The crow was too foolish to understand what the frog was doing. The frog had now started to enjoy this. He said to himself, "I haven't met a bigger fool than this crow. And to think that I was afraid of him all these years! I can amuse myself with him all day."

The crow was getting more and more nervous as he flew around. Everywhere he looked, he could only sense trouble. He began thinking of the worst possible dangers before the frog could unveil these to him. Finally, the crow landed on the ground, next to a small statue of Goddess Kali. He placed the frog on the ground but before he could eat him up, the frog began smiling.

"Oh, what now?" said the crow in an annoyed voice. The frog smiled and replied, "You see, I am a devotee of

Goddess Kali and she will not allow any harm done unto me right in front of her eyes." The crow picked up the frog and flew away once more.

By this time, the crow was trembling with fear. He was running out of options. He had to do something. As time passed, he grew hungrier. He couldn't think straight. He decided to refresh himself

with some water and landed at the pond from where he had picked up the frog.

The crow expected the frog to laugh. However, to his surprise, the frog was extremely quiet. He said to him, "What's wrong? Where's that cheeky laughter of yours now?" The frog said, "There is no laughter because I have no friends over here."

This time, the crow erupted in laughter, "Hahaha! What a foolish frog you are! It's your own home and you don't have friends over here who can help you?" The frog said, "Sadly, no. I am completely at your mercy."

There was a huge grin on the crow's face. Finally, he was going to enjoy his meal. But before he could, the frog asked him, "I have a small request. Can you please sharpen your beak before you pierce my body? That way my death will be less painful." The now arrogant crow said, "Why should I care whether your death is painful or not?"

The frog went down on his knees and

pleaded. "Have you forgotten that I warned you not once but thrice when your life was in danger? You owe me this one last request." The crow thought about it and agreed. He said to the frog, "Don't you move from here. I will be right back," and flew to the pond to wet his beak.

Then he would whet it on a slab nearby to make his beak as sharp as an arrow.

As soon as the crow flew to the pond, the quick-witted frog jumped into the pond and saved himself. He had learnt the lesson to never venture out in the open ever again.

Meanwhile, the crow couldn't stop thinking about his meal. Soon, he was done sharpening his beak. "I hope it's true what they say: A hard-earned meal

tastes even more delicious. Ah! I cannot control my excitement anymore!" he said to himself. Then he turned around, only to find that the frog was gone. Even then, he did not realise what had happened. He started calling out to the frog, "Come out, my friend! My beak is extremely sharp now! It's sharper than a sword's edge!"

The frog lifted his face out of the pond and said, "Good! Now you can start sharpening your wits!"

The Tiger and the Jackal

Deep in the Himalayan jungles, there lived a white jackal who was quite different from his pack. While the rest of the jackals feasted on other animals, the white jackal preferred to live off fruits and berries. He was a kind and

truthful jackal, whereas the other jackals were greedy, cruel and cunning. The white jackal had decided to live a life of solitude away from the rest of his pack and other animals.

Upon seeing this, the other jackals got quite annoyed. They thought to themselves, "This jackal thinks too highly of himself. He eats simple berries while we feast on this deer? This behaviour is unacceptable. Every animal must remain true to its nature. That's the circle of life." After an elaborate discussion, the other jackals decided to go and school the white jackal and try to change his perspective.

When they went to him, one of the jackals said, "Hey friend, the way in which you live is not acceptable to us. We don't like it. If it's too much of a hassle for you, we will give you some of the meat we hunt. You don't have to

live like this."

The white jackal was humble and calm. He replied, "Thank you for your kind concern. However, I am happy living on just fruit."

The other jackals didn't like this response. One of them said, "Do you think that by imitating other animals, you are better than all of us?"

The jackal was well aware of his position in the forest's hierarchy. Yet, he didn't want his low position to lower his conduct.

One of the other jackals heard this and said, "That's complete nonsense! You don't get to decide on your conduct. The way we live has been laid down by our forefathers generations ago. We jackals have to merely follow the rules." The white jackal refuted this. He said, "My dear friends, if we are responsible

for our actions then isn't it true that we have complete control and choice over our actions?"

Meanwhile, King Tiger, the king of the forest, was eavesdropping on this conversation. Upon hearing the white jackal's words, he knew that he was a learned animal with blameless conduct.

The conversation between the jackals continued. The white jackal grew tired of the arguments and impositions of his friends and said, "My friends, I do not wish to lead your kind of life. It is evil that leads one towards temptation and discontent. I am happy the way I am." The other jackals gave up and decided to leave the white jackal alone.

The king knew that this jackal was quite unusual and deserved the utmost respect. Once the other jackals had left, King Tiger approached the

white jackal with an offer. He said to him, "O righteous soul, I overheard your conversation with the other jackals. I respect you for your honourable sentiments. Please come to my court and become my Chief Minister. Your wisdom will be truly appreciated there."

The white jackal looked blank. There wasn't a hint of expression on his face. He thought for a while and said, "O mighty king, thank you for your most generous offer. However, I do not wish to live the luxurious life of a courtier. I have also never served anyone and I am quite happy where I am now."

The tiger was not one to take no for an answer. He continued to persuade the white jackal.

After a while, the jackal said, "If you are so determined to appoint me, I will obey. However, you must treat my advice with respect and allow me to

give it to you in private." Without any hesitation, the king agreed.

And so, the white jackal was appointed as King Tiger's Chief Minister. He was treated with utmost respect. At first, the other animals were not too keen on trusting him. However, as time passed, they confided in him and soon began to trust him with all their problems. The jackal was not only witty, he was also wise and just. He managed to solve the animals' problems with ease.

Everyone respected his decisions. The white jackal made sure that the animals got justice. However, the other jackals in the forest remained untrusting of the white jackal. They grew tired and angry. The jackals conspired together.

The leader of the jackals said to the pack, "That white jackal is one of us! Why must he help those common animals? Through

his decisions, he has sent our friends to jail. We must do something about it!" Just then, one of the jackals came up with a plan to get rid of the white jackal by discrediting him.

One young jackal amongst the pack didn't

wish to harm the white jackal. The white jackal had always been a friend to him. However, he knew that if he objected, the other jackals would harm him too. So, he just went along with the plan.

One day, the jackals sneaked into the king's dining room. There, they found his dinner lying on the table, waiting for him. They stealthily placed the king's dinner in the white jackal's room.

When the king entered the dining room, he was furious to see his plate empty. He screamed, "WHO DARED TO TOUCH MY PLATE BEFORE I ATE?! SPEAK UP!" Just then, the jackals came in and said to him, "It wasn't us, Your Majesty.

But, we saw the Chief Minister take the meat to his room." King Tiger couldn't believe it. He had to see for himself.

He went to the Chief Minister's room to find his dinner lying there. His anger knew no bounds. He screamed, "How can I ever trust anyone ever again? I thought he was an honest and simple jackal. What a fool I was! The Chief Minister needs to be executed at once!" He then ordered his guards to arrest him.

However, the young jackal couldn't bear to see his friend behind bars. He knew he had to do something about it. He went to the king secretly and told him everything that his evil jackal friends

had plotted against the white jackal. The king realised his mistake and asked for the white jackal to be released at once.

The white jackal was called before the king. King Tiger said to the white jackal, "Friend, I was wrong to make such a hasty decision. Kindly resume your duties." The jackal was not happy to hear this. He said,

"Your Majesty, first you bestowed upon me one of the highest honours and then you treated me as your enemy. I cannot work for you anymore."

The king was disheartened. He said, "Please forgive me. I should have judged you based on your actions, which have always been just. I should have questioned myself and given you a chance to redeem yourself. I let my anger get the better of me."

The white jackal replied, "Trust once lost cannot be regained. Such a scar permanently marks relationships. Please give me your permission to go away." The king had no other choice but to relieve the white jackal of his duties.

The white jackal left and spent the rest of his days in the forest in complete solitude.

BUDDHIST STORIES
FUNNY FOLKTALES
TALES OF WIT AND WISDOM
AMAZING FOLKTALES from South Asia
AMAR CHITRA KATHA
FASCINATING STORIES from India
AMAR CHITRA KATHA
UNUSUAL FABLES from India
AMAR CHITRA KATHA
FABULOUS FABLES from India
AMAR CHITRA KATHA
JATAKA TALES
AMAR CHITRA KATHA
WITTY MINISTER STORIES
AMAR CHITRA KATHA
STORIES FROM THE PANCHATANTRA
AMAR CHITRA KATHA
ROYAL FANTASY STORIES
AMAR CHITRA KATHA
FAVOURITE INDIAN FOLKTALES
AMAR CHITRA KATHA

ABOUT ACK

Amar Chitra Katha was founded in 1967 and is a household name in India. It is synonymous with the visual reinvention of the quintessentially Indian stories from the great epics, mythology, history, literature, oral folktales and many other sources.

With a heavy bent on authenticity and meticulous research, Amar Chitra Katha prides itself on being the most informative and trusted storyteller for children. The stories in this series have been adapted directly from the comics for young readers.

Today, Amar Chitra Katha is a cultural phenomenon, custodian of more than 400 comics in 20+ languages that have sold 100+ million copies to date. Amar Chitra Katha is available in bookstores, online and across digital platforms.